The Check Is

NOT

in the Mail

Leonard Sklar

Baroque Publishing) c 1990
San Mateo, California

Typesetting by Compositors
Copyediting by Eva Strock
Production by Rosaleen Bertolino, Bookman Productions
Book and jacket design by Renee Deprey, Bookman Productions

Baroque Publishing
4 West Fourth Avenue
Suite 501
San Mateo, CA 94402

ISBN 0-9624833-5-4

Library of Congress Catalog Card Number 89-82041

90 91 92 93   10 9 8 7 6 5 4 3 2 1

WARNING - DISCLAIMER

ii

About the Author

———

Leonard Sklar has been writing for more than thirty-three years, combining his education in economics with his experience in the business world, including thirteen years with Proctor and Gamble, Dow Chemical, IBM, and Computer Dynamics. In 1970 he founded a collection agency in San Francisco, motivated by an overwhelming desire to start and manage a company—almost *any* company. Sklar felt that a collection agency was a good business to start because it required little capital and the industry was backward enough, at that time, to be susceptible to the ministrations of an experienced businessman.

He quickly got his comeuppance from several dozen competitors unimpressed with his intentions for taking business from them. Thus he began an innovative program of collection seminars—four a year—in which he taught participants how to prevent collection problems and collect more accounts themselves. Through this scheme a goodly percentage of each audience decided that Len was a good guy to do business with. Even businesses that had never been brave enough to use a collection agency for slow-paying debtors were encouraged to use him.

Sklar began presenting seminars in other cities, and by

1982, when he sold his agency, he was conducting more than 400 seminars a year in 220 cities in all 50 states, using a group of 9 seminar presenters who he had trained. Now in his twenty-first year in this field, Sklar has become a nationally known expert in the psychology and technique of communicating about money.

In addition to seminars, Sklar has produced workbooks, audio cassettes and videocassette programs, flipcharts, newletters, and a 250-page self-study learning course on collections. This book is the culmination of his education activities in the field. He loved writing it and is currently threatening to write at least two more books, one on cooking for people who hate to do it, and a novel with a risque title.

Preface

_____

This book was written for the millions of businesses, especially small entrepreneurial ones, that want to grow and prosper by serving their customers well but that also expect to be paid promptly for their product or service. In my thirty-two years of business experience, including the past twenty years as a specialist in the psychology and strategy of collecting, I've observed a universal fear among people in business: They want the money they've earned, but they're deeply afraid to press too hard lest they upset customers who not only might not pay but could also take their business elsewhere and, for good measure, tell all their friends how nasty that business was. That fear needs to be taken seriously, even by giant corporations with similar concerns.

With the benefit gained from helping thousands of businesspeople all around the United States, in both large and very small cities, I felt that I could contribute to the literature of collecting. I observed that most writers on collection matters like a relatively mechanistic approach. That is, they'll tell you about the various kinds of debtors, the different incentives that motivate people to pay, and the ways of communicating these messages to debtors. They'll also provide excellent legal forms and information.

I believe that these approaches are helpful but much too simplistic. What must be added are these questions (and answers):

1. What do you do if the debtor *isn't* motivated as he "should" be?
2. How do you learn to listen to what a debtor is really saying (or not saying) versus what words he's mouthing?
3. How do you learn to handle any type of resistance to being financially responsible?
4. How do you get your company to create and communicate a clear payment policy to all customers so that they know exactly the rules of the game?
5. How do you get sales and credit working together?
6. How do you keep the boss from interfering in credit granting or collection matters when that's damaging to the business?

These and other questions are psychological in origin. Facts and systems alone won't give satisfactory answers. Here's another question. How can you ask for money effectively and confidently when you're usually uncomfortable in doing so? Many people are very uncomfortable about asking for payment, and the typical solutions usually don't provide relief.

The Check Is Not in the Mail can be used as a training guide for salespeople as well as for managers and collectors. The book shows how similar selling and collecting are. However, in the real world, sales gets most of the attention, and collection doesn't. Yet collection problems can sink a business. They're a symptom of a systemic, attitudinal fear of how the business is positioned in the marketplace. Collection problems that are systematically addressed affect a business as much as improved sales.

With this point of view, I intend that this book become a new standard in the field of business and education. If I'm lucky enough to have that happen, it's because of the help, encouragement, and advice of many people and institutions, starting with my alma mater, Franklin and Marshall College in Lancaster, Pennsylvania. The school gave me a superb liberal arts education that encouraged me to be open to, and to synthesize, ideas from many sources. My five years at Proctor and Gamble gave me an awareness of marketing as well as experience in industrial engineering. My years at IBM taught me invaluable lessons about selling, overcoming resistance, and the common elements of the broad variety of businesses I dealt with.

I want to thank many people, beginning with my wife, Marcia, who's always supportive of all of my activities and who thought that a book was the best idea ever.

Helen Mann, my assistant, manager, and executive secretary for eighteen years, had to take hundreds of pages of my handwritten scratching and make English sentences out of them for the word processor. She did so, as always, with incredible skill and patience.

Arthur Friedman taught me an approach to dealing with people that's the most unbelievable I've ever heard. He taught me how to win more by being willing to lose a few. His philosophy of interacting with people allowed me to learn and teach roleplaying in a way that the player never has to worry about what to say and always wins in the encounter.

I am indebted to my friend and business partner, Bob Morris, for insights on sound business techniques as well as information on commercial accounts. Bob and Arthur are both ideal business associates and friends who I trust implicitly.

I am grateful to Jared Heim, Bob Tessler, Chuck Tuckman, and Bill Levin, all of whom reviewed the book prior to printing and offered some valuable insights and corrections. As experienced businessmen, they helped keep the writing clear and to the point.

My thanks also to Jay Levinson, who made key suggestions for the book title.

Tom Nerney, Craig Wollner, Mike Crisp, Dan Poynter, and

Jeff Herman gave me an education in the business of writing and publishing. Charley and Marcia Chase were quick to help with their excellent examples of financial policy for attorneys.

I hope you get as much enjoyment from reading this book as I had writing it. Although I've written articles and manuals, the act of creating a book was a new and wonderful experience.

As I see it, once you've read my book, we have a relationship. I'd love to hear from you. Write to me at this address: Leonard Sklar, 4 West Fourth Avenue, Suite 501, San Mateo, California 94402.

Read on and enjoy.

Contents

1

What's the Big Deal About Collecting?

Money evokes strong feelings. A sign in one company office reads "The End of the World Is Coming. Please Pay Your Bill So We Don't Have To Chase All Over Hell For You!" Cute? Sure. Serious? Not really, but the sign does express the feeling, even if nobody would ever act that way.

In some circles, money matters so much that if you don't pay your debt, you get your legs broken—or worse. And the poorest odds in a gambling casino are with the game of Keno. But because the payoff from gambling can be huge, greed, hope, or desperation let the mind forget the odds, as do the state lotteries.

These examples illustrate that money matters deeply. And collecting money for a product or service provided is serious business. Let's be specific. To a business, collecting means getting paid—in full, on time, and without hassles. Accounts receivable is usually the second largest tangible asset of any business, after plant and equipment. Collecting that money is a major concern.

Thus this book isn't about collecting art, fine wines, paper clips, dust, or any other things people sometimes collect. We're talking *money* here: the medium of exchange, the measure of who's winning, the litmus test of success, the evidence of survival, the distinction between the haves and the have-nots. Money is a *very* big deal. Willie Sutton, a notorious bank robber in the 1940s and 1950s, when asked why he robbed banks, replied simply, "Because that's where the money is." No obscure psychological explanation for Willie.

To get money, a legitimate business has to give something in return, a product or service of value to the buyer. For a business, getting the money can present major obstacles. (Chapter 2 analyzes the main reasons for the obstacles.) The magnitude, persistence, and complexity of the problem prevent businesses, large and small, profit-making or nonprofit, from achieving their full potential. Not only that, it's *irritating* when you get stiffed! Surprisingly, the nature of collection problems is pretty much the same for both small and large businesses. You'd think that the larger, more established companies would have the experience and the systems in place to spot and correct collection snags before they occur; but this isn't the case.

My 20 years of consulting for and training of every type of business has provided a simple explanation. The common denominator is *people*. Regardless of the size of the company, business is *people interacting with other people*, and human beings express themselves in a variety of ways. The exchange of money for products and services is *not* a mechanical process. Even with clear and complete written credit and collection policies, breaking or bending the rules can be justified easily. Even cash businesses, such as movie theaters and fast-food restaurants, although they essentially have no collection problems, experiment with new ways of getting their money. For example, some of these establishments are now accepting credit cards as a way of increasing sales.

To illustrate how large, sophisticated businesses can take leave of their senses regarding collection policy and procedures, consider all the money center banks that have loaned billions to countries whose credit-worthiness is quite dubious. The savings and loans invested in ever riskier investments in the hopes of paying for the higher and higher interest rates they offered to attract depositors. And numerous colleges and universities can't collect defaulted student loans. The list could go on and on. So don't tell me that bigger, older businesses have more protection from collection problems. There's no evidence to back you up.

Small businesses, which can least afford the drain on cash flow, feel the pinch even more than the big guys when their collections are slow. According to Dun & Bradstreet's survey of 9 million companies, firms with fewer than 10 employees are the last to get paid; they take on riskier accounts and lack the resources for effective collection of debts.

Thus, not only do collection problems cut across large and small, new and established businesses, they occur with equal ferocity in all parts of the country. People often say, "We're different." People think small towns are different from big cities. The South is different from the East and the Midwest. Rural is different from urban. Nonsense. Of course there are some noticeable differences among people, but the common elements are thoughts and feelings and a common, marvelous variety of humanity. I bring up this fact because some businesspeople avoid confronting their real collection problems by denial, by saying "we're different."

In the hierarchy of business functions, collections is not a major player. It tends to be part of the controller's job and doesn't hold a candle to sales, research, production, marketing, advertising, or other business departments as far as status is concerned. Collection people feel acutely the low status both the company and society confer on them. When asked at a social gathering "What do you do," the collection people usually mumble something about financial management or some other euphemism. Used car salespeople have about as much status, maybe more. How many heads of companies do you know who came up through the collection ranks?

On the other hand, chief executives are acutely aware of

the *importance* of collecting, because they watch their accounts receivable closely. What may not be clear to them is how to best manage those receivables in the light of the company's other goals, such as growth, new products, and diversification.

To some businesspeople, the way to deal with collection worries is to finesse them by selling more! But that's almost like the gambling system that calls for doubling the bet each time you lose. That last bet can wipe you out; don't do it!

Let's compare selling to collecting, based on a business that earns a 20 percent profit before taxes (PBT) on sales. Start with a $1000 sale that, if paid for, results in a $200 PBT. Suppose the buyer doesn't pay. What are the choices for replacing that $200 profit?

1. Invest another $1000 to produce a comparable sale and the resulting $200 profit.
2. Invest $100 in a collection effort to get paid for the original sale and pocket the same profit.

This example is simplistic, but the comparison is valid, pointing to the need for clear, analytical thinking about two key business issues:

1. How much should be invested in the credit and collection functions?
2. What should the company policy on granting and enforcing credit be?

Conclusion: Money isn't everything, but it isn't nothing, either.

2

Why You Really Have Collection Problems, and What to Do About Them

Do unpaid bills just go with the territory, or can you do something about them? The answers are yes and yes. If businesses have control over their receivables, and they do, the beginning of wisdom is to find out why these problems occur. This approach leads to *prevention* rather than constant fixing of problems.

Here's an insight you may not like: The collection problems you have aren't done unto you by others. You aren't a victim.

You cause all your own collection problems. Therefore only you can clean them up. This is a pretty rough statement. You may not agree with me on this point, but to the extent you disagree, you'll needlessly continue having excessive receivables. Here then are the five chief causes of collection problems in business.

Fear of Loss of Business

This is the biggest single reason why businesses have collection problems. The fear first occurs when deciding whether or not to grant credit and how much; it reappears after the transaction, when trying to collect payment. The fear is that pressing a customer too hard to pay may result in the loss of that customer. We analyze the credit-granting part of this problem in Chapter 7. The fundamental fear is that if you don't grant liberal credit terms, you may not get the business. Some businesses have very clear, firm policies on granting credit, but many don't.

The other extreme of the business relationship is the question of how hard to push a customer who's creatively avoiding paying. The question usually causes a major psychological conflict: You want your money, but you don't want to lose the customer. Naturally, many customers are aware of this ambivalence and threaten to take their business elsewhere if you aren't reasonable. There is a big piece of evidence proving that businesses have a conflict about how hard to press for payment: *The average business holds on to unpaid accounts nine to ten months, which is twice as long as necessary for a rational, logical, economic policy!*

Most businesses would agree that they know, or could know, where they stand with most unpaid accounts after three or four months, and they could resolve them then either by writing them off or turning them over to some third party for collection. The additional six months that the typical business waits before resolving the account represents the fear of loss of business. Six months is a long time to wait to resolve a fear, particularly a fear that persists year after year. A business friend of mine used to deal with slow-paying customers by telling them, "Joe, I don't intend to carry your account more months than your mother carried you!"

If you have a good credit policy and a customer pays in an unsatisfactory manner for four months, and you take strong measures that result in your losing that customer, the odds are that you're *better off* cutting your losses early. You probably would have lost the customer anyway, so waiting longer only prolongs your agony and your costs. Professional gamblers know that you have to "know when to hold 'em and when to fold 'em." Amateurs, living more in a fantasy world, don't know when to fold 'em, so they keep betting and wind up losing more.

Absence of, or Unclear, Collection Policy

A high percentage of businesses have no clearly formulated payment policy. They know it, they're embarrassed to admit it, and they're slow to deal with the problem even when they acknowledge its importance. Why?

Some businesses fear that if they put a policy in writing, they'll be locked into a rigid approach to doing business, one that doesn't allow appropriate stretching of the rules when necessary. No problem. All that are required are an *external* policy that spells out the rules for all customers to go by and an *internal* policy that explains what to do for customers who require a bending of the rules. Customers don't get to see the internal policy. In other words, the internal policy prescribes the backoff steps; the external policy spells out what you're backing away from. It's a great combination.

Many businesses look at a payment policy from one of the following points of view:

1. Have a clear, unambiguous, no-nonsense policy that lets customers know exactly what the rules are. The result is few collection problems, but also fewer customers.

2. Have an ambiguous or nonexistent payment policy. The result is plenty of grateful customers but a ruinous load of unpaid accounts.

Many businesses *think* that these are the only two viewpoints, neither of which makes for a profitable business.

Actually, the right kind of policy, internal as well as external, lets a business have its cake and eat it too. Such a policy both encourages growth and keeps accounts receivable to a minimum. We show how to set up a collection policy in Chapter 6.

Lack of Status, Training, or Career Path for Collection Personnel

A few companies, but only a few, have accorded their collection activities the kind of attention and investment that they eagerly devote to advertising, sales, or any number of other functions. These companies provide extensive, professional, continuous training, state-of-the-art technology, detailed measurement of results, incentives, and a career path for their people. But far too few businesses offer these benefits or, at best, a computer system for recordkeeping. Yet training is available for everyone. Technology for recordkeeping, account management, automatic phone dialing, and more is available and becoming more sophisticated. The return on investment from a professional collection function is incredibly high. Viewed strictly from the standpoint of margins, it makes much sense for a business to invest more in collecting.

Reluctance to Use Outside Collection Services

Some business owners don't find much excitement in collections, so they direct their attention to other aspects of the business. In any business, the boss can't be good at everything, so focusing on one's strengths makes sense. Even so, if receivables are bad and there is no internal mechanism to deal with them, the solution is obvious: get outside professional help. After all, you can't be an expert in everything.

Available help includes collection attorneys, small claims courts, collection temporaries, collection agencies, and collection letter services.

As we saw, businesses hold on to accounts an average of nine to ten months, six months longer than they should. A big reason is *ego*. If an outside service collects the accounts, the inside staff look bad, or so the company thinks. If the outside service does poorly, the insiders may look good, but the accounts may have been overworked, which is bad. Confusing? Not really—it simply indicates the need for a systematic approach to account management, which requires resolution of accounts and placement with an outside service much more quickly, and considers ego considerations irrelevant.

Businesses also avoid the professional outsider because of *cost*, which appears to be an unnecessary, added cost that can be minimized by working longer on the accounts in-house. This analysis ignores not only the added internal costs but the fact that time spent working on fresher accounts is far more productive than hacking away on older ones.

Policies of Other Companies

If you operate a small business and your customers include other businesses, perhaps a company like DuPont, IBM, or a U.S. government agency, you can have whatever policy you like, but you'll do business by the *other* company's policy. As long as you know their policy going in, you can choose to accept their rules or move on. This is the only collection problem that you have limited control over, particularly if your big company customer is arbitrary in paying you or if they change the rules along the way.

As for the other causes of collection problems, you have the ability to change and control them all. It's not easy, but any business can do it. The tough message is that the insights you need, all of which are in this book, and the changes necessary to get the results you want are often difficult to acquire and put into practice. The good news is that you have control over the process and the changes can be made quickly. You can see results in just a few months.

Conclusion: Changing unworkable collection policies is best done all at once rather than a little at a time. Nobody likes too much change, so you might as well be done with the trauma all at once rather than suffer the death of 1000 cuts.

3

The Art of Collecting Revealed

Here we look directly at what collecting is, what it isn't, and what it's like. The analogies help us come to grips with the full impact of how collection awareness can improve company profit and growth.

To become a pro in mastering collections, you need to know four key analogies:

1. Collecting is *negotiation*.
2. Collecting is *selling*.
3. Collecting is *percentages*.
4. Collecting is a *game*.

I intend to examine each analogy thoroughly so you can understand the solid reasons for developing the detailed credit and collection policy you need to serve your profit and growth objectives. In other words, without fully reconnoitering the enemy's position, strength, firepower, and plans, your army can't produce its own winning battle plan. The military analogy is apt because your debtors—the enemy—aren't on your side; they're pervasive, they use deception when they can, they'll bide their time looking for an opportunity to strike, and if they have superior firepower, they'll overwhelm you. It's a war out there! If you don't collect what's owed to you, you won't win this war.

Collecting Is Negotiation

Collecting is negotiation because any time a debtor (customer, client, patient, or borrower) doesn't pay you—in full, on time, and without hassles—you're in a negotiation. The debtor wants to delay payment, but you want it all now. You not only need to know how to negotiate, you also need to be instantly aware that you're in a negotiation.

Courses and books on negotiation are widely available. Among the leading authors in the field are Chester Karass and Gerald Nierenberg. They, as well as most other specialists in the subject, propose that both sides in a negotiation should win; one side shouldn't win at the other's expense. If you persuade a debtor to pay more than he intended, he may end up feeling that he underwent a medical procedure called a payectomy, whereby money is extracted, which leaves a gaping wound, blood on the floor, and much ill will and pain. We have no intention of conducting such a win-lose negotiation. We want win-win. What can we offer a debtor who ends the negotiation by paying more than he intended?

1. Self-respect for being responsible.
2. Freedom from a collection agency or attorney.
3. Appreciation for your bending the rules for him (which is one very good reason for having a clearly stated credit and collection policy).
4. Willingness to counsel the debtor on ways of getting money to pay you as well as other creditors.

There are more benefits you can offer, but you get the point.

A win-win negotiation can offer both sides elements of predictability, as often happens in the sale of a house. The seller typically puts the house on the market at a price higher than he expects to get; the buyer offers a lowball price. Then the seller and buyer haggle, usually winding up somewhere between the high asking price and the low initial offer—*and both sides are fully aware of the game,* or should be.

This is why we value compromise so much: *It leaves everyone's ego intact.* A good negotiation is one in which both sides are equally unhappy at the end. Certain human qualities are found almost everywhere, in almost everyone, including the desire for a bargain. We all love a good deal *regardless of how much money we have.* You just don't want your debtor to have the good deal at your expense. The debtor will try, and you can even acknowledge the professional bargain-hunting debtor as being a great negotiator. But as you skillfully use all the payment strategies presented in Chapter 8, your negotiation skills will give you the best possible collection result.

Collecting Is Selling

In a selling situation, a sale is always made: either the salesperson sells the prospect on buying, or the prospect sells the salesperson on the fact that no sale is going to be made now. Collecting is so much like selling that any collector can get better by taking a professional sales course or reading some good sales training literature. Four key sales concepts and skills that a professional collector must have are (1) qualify the prospect, (2) acknowledge resistance, (3) keep records, and (4) be a closer. Let's look at each idea in detail.

Qualify the Prospect

Based on what the prospect says and does, the salesperson has to decide whether or not the prospect is going to buy. If the answer is a flat *no* and the sales potential is small, it makes sense to walk away and see someone else. But if the prospect says, "Tell me more," there's reason to invest more time. And the main issue is time. Just as no salesperson can spend equal amounts of time with all prospects or clients, no collector can spend equal time with all debtors.

As does the salesperson, the collector *must* make decisions constantly about time investments, but complete information is never available. The professional salesperson or collector also has to ask the prospect or debtor probing questions. An evasive answer is useful for shortening the time spent. But even a direct answer has to be listened to with a "third ear," to determine if the prospect or debtor is simply saying what he thinks the listener wants to hear.

Acknowledge Resistance

The professional salesperson usually knows, from experience, the main reasons why a prospect doesn't buy, including: "I don't need it"; "Your price is too high"; "Your terms aren't good enough"; "I get top service now"; "Your specs are off"; "You don't have the delivery time I need"; and countless more. Knowing what the objections to buying are likely to be, the salesperson brings up these resistance points herself and then answers each one in turn. If this tactic isn't used, the prospect can easily decide not to buy because of some reason that the prospect hasn't brought up and that then hasn't been put to rest by the salesperson.

The collector must also master the classic types of resistance to paying (called excuses) that debtors typically use. Although the collector doesn't initiate a discussion of excuses, his acknowledgement of them when the debtor presents them is essential in resolving the account. If the collector doesn't acknowledge the excuses, the debtor's resistance will persist.

Keep Records

Great natural salespeople are sometimes terrible record-keepers, and vice versa. Good verbal skills with a prospect aren't enough. The professional salesperson also keeps detailed sales call records, makes believable sales projections, does prospect research, writes proposals and reports in clear, readable English, and plans and manages his activities to control the territory and himself.

Similarly, the professional collector documents each call, can instantly retrieve any account, can whip through skiptracing resources quickly and productively, and plans and manages an inventory of 500 to 2000 accounts. Fortunately, as the technology for handling the recordkeeping and account management aspects of collecting keeps improving, the time available for collectors to be on the phone with a debtor, which is where collectors are most productive, goes up substantially. Computers today provide paperless account control, automatic letter generation, account selection, client reports, and more. Automated phone systems make the calls, assign them to a collector to handle when the debtor answers, keep trying when a busy signal occurs, and keep track of the time and cost by account, collector, or client.

Be a Closer

Horror stories in sales literature include the salesperson who "makes the sale and then buys it back." In other words, after clinching the sale, the seller kept talking about new points that made the buyer change her mind. When the collection is made, a slightly different approach is needed: Nail down the commitment. Confirm when the money will be sent, in what amount, to what address, and, sometimes, by whom.

Salespeople also learn trial closes—questions that indicate whether a buying decision has been made. For example, a salesperson may ask, "If you were to install one of our machines, would it be Model 400 or 800?" If the prospect answers either model, the sales is moving to a conclusion. Of course, if the prospect says "neither," much more selling, qualifying, and trial closing is needed. For the collector, trial closes come right away and repeatedly. The best opening line for the collection sale is to ask for payment in full today—no beating around the bush. If the debtor "buys," great; a "sale" has been made. If the debtor balks, the negotiating, and more trial closes, begins.

There are more comparisons between collecting and selling, but the ones cited here should make it clear that the time, money, and training most companies invest in sales can also produce wonderful results if collections receive more attention than usual.

Collecting Is Percentages

Sellers and collectors both have to play the numbers right. For many years, Babe Ruth was known as the man who hit more home runs per season than anyone else. What was not so well known is that he also struck out more than anyone. What made this paradox possible was that he came to bat so often.

Suppose the average salesperson makes one sale in ten calls, and she makes ten calls a day. The professional salesperson, on the other hand, might make twenty calls a day. If the closing ratio is only 1 in 10, that's still two sales a day. The pro strikes out eighteen times, which is twice the average, but she also makes two sales a day instead of one. Instead of taking the eighteen nos as personal rejections, the pro rejoices in having found eighteen prospects that she no longer has to expect very much from.

Collectors need to deal with rejection and stress also. But the professional collector learns that the more contacts made, the more money comes in, whatever the skill level. Playing the percentages means "coming to bat" as often as possible. A rejection is just one less person to invest much time in. As you'll read more than once in this book, you have to accept the need to hold 'em sometimes and fold 'em other times. The courage is in the informed decision to fold 'em, regardless of how current the account is. If the account is two weeks old and you have a complete skip, get rid of it right away. There's no benefit in waiting a few months before writing off the account or assigning it to some outsider collector.

Collecting Is a Game

A game is a form of negotiation, only it isn't legitimate or honorable in purpose. Haven't you said of someone, "They're playing games with me!", and you didn't mean it as a compliment? Debtors play a wondrous variety of games, sometimes consciously but often unconsciously, sort of like going on automatic pilot. For example, some older people, when asked to pay, play the "little old person" game, in which they try to convince the collector that anyone over sixty couldn't possibly understand why they have to pay the bill.

My favorite true story about game playing concerns a doctor in Beverly Hills who had been in practice almost fifty years and had mostly wealthy patients who paid their bills an average of eighteen months after treatment. (The wealthy can certainly find better things to do with money than pay bills to a doctor who doesn't ask for payment.) The doctor's permissive policy put him on the verge of bankruptcy, and he didn't have enough money put aside to retire. So he was really in a tough spot; he *had* to change his policy, even though, naturally, he was afraid his patients would all go elsewhere if he insisted on faster payment.

In desperation, the doctor brought in a business manager who was experienced in such a situation. She said, "Doctor, what payment policy would you like from now on?" After sweating uncomfortably for a while, the doctor finally said, "What I'd *really* like is to be paid in full at the time of treatment and for all my present patients to bring their outstanding bills current. But, if I did that, they'd be upset, go elsewhere, probably to a much younger doctor, and I'd be worse off than I am now."

The business manager told the doctor, "No problem. If you agree to practice medicine and let me handle the payments, without interceding if a patient comes running to you, I promise you will turn this practice around." Not really having much choice, the doctor said, "Go ahead." The office manager was instructed to tell each patient, as they came in for their next visit, "We have a new policy. From now on, upon the advice of doctor's CPA, all outstanding bills must be taken care of, in full, and all future visits are to be paid for at the time of treatment." The office manager did so. At that point, she said, every one of those patients, most of whom were women, went into their "indignant matron" game. They drew themselves up to their full height, their face and body formed into a frozen mask, looked down their nose with no effort to conceal contempt and deep offense, and said, in effect, "How dare you, you miserable worm, question my ability to pay this bill? I will certainly tell all my friends how heartless this office has become."

Most office personnel, when confronted with that onslaught, will back up fast. But this office manager knew it was coming, so she simply looked each indignant matron square in the eyes and stated, calmly and evenly, "Oh, there's no question whatever about your ability to pay this bill. That's why we're delighted to have you remain in the practice, if you so choose. But the policy of the office now is as I've stated it."

What happened? Some of the patients, seeing that their game wasn't going to work, stomped out of the office. A few stayed away permanently, but most came quietly back when they realized that no one was buying their game. Most of the patients simply blinked and paid up.

The office manager said that she learned three valuable lessons from that experience. Lesson 1. Those patient debtors who try to dominate, manipulate, and dump guilt will do so to *anyone* they think they can manipulate. I call them equal opportunity guilt dumpers.

Lesson 2. These people not only try to manipulate and dump guilt on everyone possible, they also *look down* on anyone it works on. Their attitude is "Good, got another one."

Lesson 3. When I confronted them and stopped the game, most of them not only paid up as requested, they actually *respected* me for standing up to them.

Within a few months, even after losing a few patients, cash flow surged to unheard-of levels and the practice was busier than ever. I promise you that this drama is being played out in millions of businesses around the world. Maybe you cringed a few times while reading the story because you have a few game players like them in your business. Not to worry. Before you're finished with this book, you'll have all the weapons for spotting game players and the courage to confront them, knowing that your business, and even your customers, will be better off.

Conclusion: If you like personal growth and challenge, collecting offers you both. I suggest you broaden every employee by having them spend some training time as a collector.

4

Big, Small, Commercial, Consumer—What Kind of Business Is Yours?

Because business is conducted by people, there are very few fundamental differences between business done by big companies or small companies. You'd expect bigger, longer-established companies to have well-defined, thoroughly explained, and rigorously implemented credit and collection policies as compared to newer or smaller establishments. In some companies, that's certainly the case, but my experience has been that bigger businesses are, in general, no more professional in their payment policies and procedures than the newer or smaller ones. In fact the big guys may be worse, for two reasons:

1. Big companies are hungry for business. The need to grow relentlessly forces "flexibility" in the payment policy.
2. The market is dynamic, changing as inevitably for the big company as for the small. The whale turns more slowly than the minnow, and size is no protection from consumers' demands for the best possible deal. For

example, witness IBM's continuous thrashing to regain some control over its shifting markets and fickle customers.

Big Versus Small

In previous chapters I cited examples of very large companies that have disgraced whatever professional image they had regarding their credit policies: banks, and their disastrous loans to third world countries, colleges and their systematic noncollection of student loans, and savings and loans and their invitation to world-class plunderers to make loans that enriched only themselves.

A few minor distinctions between big and small businesses do exist:

1. If you run a small business and want to do business with, say, Du Pont or the U.S. government, even though you have a clear, written business policy, you can expect to do business by *their* policy, not yours.

2. A big business is likely to have deeper pockets, the better to absorb its credit follies without feeling the pinch so quickly.

3. A big company is more likely to be publicly owned. Even though the management may be compensated for performance, they're generally far less personally accountable than owners of small businesses, whose incomes rise or fall more directly with the fortunes of the business. On the other hand, large, debt-laden leveraged buyouts exert tremendous pressure to produce cash flow, and the management is sure to feel the urgency for collecting outstanding bills.

4. Big businesses can more easily justify investment in technology to improve the efficiency of the credit and collection people.

Commercial Versus Consumer

I now want to make some distinctions between consumer debt and commercial debt. The definition of a commercial debt, according to the American Commercial Collectors Association, is "A commercial claim arises from an obligation to pay for goods sold or leased, services rendered, or monies loaned for use in the conduct of a business or profession, and not for personal consumption." A consumer debt, therefore, is money owed by an individual to either another individual or a business.

Of U.S. debt, 20 percent is consumer debt, 80 percent is commercial. The average commercial account is four to five times larger than the consumer account—approximately $1300 versus $250. Commercial business is conducted 95 to 98 percent on credit. In consumer business, a much higher percentage is paid by cash or check rather than on credit. Consumer accounts have a broader base (more customers) and a smaller exposure (fewer dollars per account) than commercial accounts.

In collecting from consumers, a business may communicate only with the person who owes the money (or their attorney and, in many states, the spouse), whereas in collecting a commercial account, a business can talk to anyone in the debtor company about the nature of the communication. (I review specific rules on harassment in Chapter 20.)

The collection of commercial accounts is resolved more quickly than that of consumer accounts; the company is either in business or it is not. The human element plays a part here; it's often easier to press a company for payment rather than another human being, the consumer debtor, which is why professional debt collectors keep reminding themselves that

1. The collection of an account is a business transaction, not an emotional experience.

2. The collection of accounts is a lesson in mathematics, not sociology.
3. A collector who works hard won't collect as much as one who works smart.

Because a commercial account is larger than a consumer account, more credit information about it must be gathered. Both commercial and consumer creditors tend to hold on to their delinquent accounts too long.

Thus the problems in and solutions for granting credit and collecting money owed, other than the well-defined distinctions just described, aren't much different for large and small businesses or commercial and consumer creditors. These distinctions pale in comparison to the similarities which derive from human frailty. In developing solutions to collection problems, we're going to include all the systems and procedures that we can get our hands on, and we're also going to look, with unblinking clarity, at the limitations of our systems and the infinite variety of debtor resistance to our systems.

———————

Conclusion: Rising waters lift all boats equally. In the world of credit and collections, we're all in the same boat, whether we're large or small, commercial or consumer.

5

A Collection Philosophy That Works

So many of our actions derive from our belief systems. Teenagers, believing themselves immortal, don't worry much about long-term effects, so they drink too much, drive too fast, and let the sun pour down on their skins. Amateur salespeople, believing (hoping) that the big sale will come along soon, somehow, avoid the day-to-day calls, follow-up, paperwork, and other real-world activities that sustain them until the big sales do get earned. Untrained collectors operate according to fantasies and belief systems that are badly thought out or not thought about at all, such as:

1. Debtors are bad people and deserve to be verbally abused. (Remember, these are ways *not* to think.)
2. I pay my bills, or try to, and by golly, there's no reason other people can't pay theirs. If they don't have the money, don't buy! (Self-righteous)
3. Debtors are like children and should be treated as such. (Condescending)
4. The collector is in the driver's seat and has the power.

Let the debtor know real quick who's the boss and who
has all the cards. (Controlling)
5. People are basically honest and good. You should take
them at their word. (Naive)
6. Every unpaid account deserves its fair share of my
time. (Nonanalytic)
7. I don't get paid enough for what I do, and they don't
appreciate me anyway. (Self-pitying)
8. I'm going to get that SOB to pay, no matter how long it
takes! (Bruised ego)

Well, you get the idea. It isn't fair to take such cheap shots,
but the level of truth in these belief systems is serious enough
to cause collectors to both fail and become bitter about their
work. Belief systems should be realistic, produce the best collection results, and provide the greatest personal satisfaction.
I've identified the following seven philosophies, or belief
systems, that meet these criteria.

You Don't Have to Be Tough to Be a Good Collector

Being hard-nosed or tough does not a good collector make.
In fact, such an attitude makes a person less effective and in-
creases the chances for an act of harassment (defined in
Chapter 20).

Some collectors fantasize that they'd be much more effective if only they could pull out a few fingernails, break some
kneecaps, or perform some other horrors of intimidation. Actually, the best collectors *never* bully, threaten, or raise their
voices. Instead, they're clear about what the rules of the
game are, and what must be done and, if necessary, the consequences of not doing it.

We're not talking about saints or robots. We're describing
people who've learned that bullying and blustering may puff

them up for an instant but that such tactics have no value and are in fact counterproductive.

Paying Bills Is Discretionary

Your company's bill isn't your debtors' only bill. Whether businesses or individuals, your debtors always have many other bills to pay or purchases they'd like to make, and they always have to decide where their limited supply of money will go. As we'll see in Philosophy 7, these decisions aren't always made rationally.

Therefore, in order to get your debtors to pay you (instead of somebody else) in full (instead of over a long time), you must produce a condition of *urgency*. You're less likely to generate the urgency you need unless you're fully aware of your debtors' immense discretion in paying other bills. (Later in the book, when I describe your credit and collection policy and your billing and collection system, you'll see that a fundamental reason for having them so clearly defined is the need for reducing what otherwise would be massive discretion by your debtors in paying you as they see fit.)

You Can't Force Debtors to Pay— You Can, However, Resolve the Account

Here's a dash of cold water: You can't force people to pay. However, you *can* force yourself to acknowledge more quickly who'll pay and who won't. Let's look closer at this bit of hardball reality.

It isn't strictly true that you can't force a debtor to pay; legal recourse works well some of the time. But even this ultimate weapon can be invalidated for various reasons, such as:

1. Account is too small to sue.

2. Debtor can't be found, so you can't serve the suit papers.
3. No apparent assets, so a judgment would be worthless.
4. Debtor files for bankruptcy, leaving him immune to legal action.
5. A few other unpleasant realities.

Debtors may not be the least bit intimidated by your promise to sue. Experienced collectors tell many tales of warning a debtor to pay or be sued and hearing in return, "Get in line" or "Take a long walk on a short pier." So, the notion that you can force a debtor to pay through fear or intimidation just doesn't hold up enough to make it a workable collection belief. The one alternative, and the realistic one, is that you can learn to detect signals from your debtors that will indicate whether or not they intend to pay.

In other words, you can increase your awareness of people as they really are, not as you'd like them to be. Chapter 9 shows you how to evaluate your debtor more accurately via the Spectrum of Debtors. This tool is the basis for resolving an account quicker and more accurately than ever.

Have a Clear Payment Policy Up Front— Even So, You'll Lose Some Customers

This philosophy flows naturally from philosophy 2, "Paying bills is discretionary." To reduce the discretion, set out rules or the debtors will make their own rules. The best time to communicate the rules is prior to doing business. Don't tell someone after the fact something that you could have said up front, particularly when it's as important as money. In other words, no surprises. Inform before you perform. Don't you want to be treated that way too?

If your business is one in which you can't inform before you perform, discuss payment policy as soon as you can after the product or service is delivered. For example, you're driving alone and you're in an accident, leaving you unconscious alongside the road. An ambulance is called, and it takes you to a hospital. There's no way the ambulance company can tell you in advance that you have to pay for the ride, which is why ambulance companies have huge collection problems. As another example, suppose you own a landscaping company and you design the plans for a homeowner or a business, hoping for the job. The customer gets several bids, and yours doesn't win. Even worse, the customer doesn't pay for the design work because you didn't make it clear, up front, that the design work must be paid for regardless of who gets the landscaping work. Designers, writers, and other creative businesses often have collection trouble with this fact of life, but the problem is preventable if you're willing to lose some business. Spell out clear rules for paying. Some prospective customers will object and go to some other supplier who's an easier mark. Let these customers go; you're better off. There's nothing wrong with losing business when that business isn't likely to pay you.

You Can't Hurt Other People's Feelings; You Can't Even Force Niceness on Them

Here's another way that fear of loss of business interferes with clear communication. When I say you can't hurt other people's feelings, I don't mean that it's perfectly OK to be as obnoxious and unfeeling as you like. It means only that you don't *control* other people's feelings. Collectors often tell me, "I want to ask them to pay, but if I did, they might get upset, take their business elsewhere, and still not pay me." Has that thought ever occurred to you? It's a trap and it doesn't hold water.

Other collectors ask, "What's a *nice* way of asking a debtor to pay?" The nice way to say something like "Please pay this bill now, in full" is simply to say it, in plain English, without beating around the bush. What isn't nice is to hem and haw, be evasive, or avoid the communication entirely because you fear that you *might* upset the debtor. Of course you might, but it's not you who *caused* the upset; the upset is what the debtor added.

My belief that you can't even force your niceness on debtors is best illustrated by the tales of experienced collectors. They report calling up debtors on the phone, asking for the money as nicely and sweetly as possible, honey almost dripping from their voices, but the debtors slam the phone down anyway! The inexperienced collector asks, "What in the world did I say to get the phone slammed in my ear?" The pro knows that it doesn't matter how the money was requested. Plenty of debtors get real self-righteous about why they shouldn't have to pay, and they take it out on those who ask.

This philosophy requires thought as well as working through because many "sensitive" people are put in a position of collecting, and they tend to be vulnerable to the emotional games that debtors can play. We can't stop the games, but we can transcend the impulse to feel responsible for causing them. So, be sensitive—even *more* sensitive than before. But be sensitive to debtors' willingness to be, or not be, responsible about the debt. When the problem is viewed this way, you can't be "too sensitive" to ask for money. What you can do is harness that sensitivity to become even more productive.

This reason is why women are often the best collectors. Since I brought up the subject, I should acknowledge that collection agency owners, as well as professional collectors, argue constantly about whether men or women make the best collectors. Many of the women feel that they lack the men's authority. But I think that's just a convenient rationalization when a collection attempt fails. In my experience, either men or women can be fantastic collectors.

You'll Win More By Being Willing to Lose a Few

The operative word here is "willing." You don't plan to lose a collection attempt; you intend to get paid. But because collecting is partly a numbers game, in which you have to make decisions about how much time to spend on an account, when it appears that you're going to lose, give it up and go on to an account that better justifies your time.

This philosophy is easy to espouse, and it's valid, but it flies in the face of another philosophy we've all been taught from childhood, namely, never give up: Try, try again. As kids, we learned about the little engine that could and the spider that spun its web for the twelfth time after it was blown away eleven times. Vince Lombardi taught us that "winning is everything." We know that nobody loves a loser. Yet, here I come telling you that, in collecting, plenty of times your best move is to give up. Even professional collection agency collectors, if pressed, admit that they hang on to unpaid accounts too long. Agency managers must constantly monitor the collectors to see that they close out the uncollectibles and work on the accounts with some life still in them.

Throughout this book, you'll see that collection success is more psychology than technique. You need the systems and techniques, but you also need to develop the willingness to use the techniques and to handle the inevitable resistance that arises. Without these insights and superior collection philosophies, you'll lose more often than you need to.

Logic Is Good, But Don't Count on It

In Chapter 15, one of the communication tools I discuss is the use of the left brain and the right brain. The left brain is the logical part and the right brain is the emotional half. An awareness of both sides of the brain is essential for a collection philosophy. There's no avoiding the need to be rational, logical, analytical, and even cold-blooded in seeing things as they are.

Without a fully functioning left brain, you may try to fly or walk on water, hope that your lotto ticket has a sure chance of winning the jackpot, and believe in other fantasies. We can't live without being rational, but we aren't Dr. Spock either. We aren't *only* logical. The emotional, intuitive part of us all is equally essential to living. In collecting, the right brain is the part that gives you the willingness to use your logic, recognizes when logic isn't working, and lets you know quickly when resistance to paying is being expressed, what to do about it, and what the odds for success will be.

That's a pretty powerful set of tools for a non-logical part of the body. We'll use all those tools in collecting.

Conclusion: Philosophy isn't just the subject that puts us to sleep in school. In collecting, the right philosophies make you a winner.

6

Collection Policy— It's a Must!

Every writer on the subject of collections insists that a business must have a collection policy, sometimes called a financial policy or a credit and collection policy. I insist also, and I'm going into detail about it so that you'll know exactly why you should have one and how to implement one.

Small businesses are notoriously guilty of having a weak or nonexistent collection policy or, if they have one, they tend to use it inconsistently, with disastrous results. Bigger companies are more likely to have well thought-out and implemented policies, but in my experience they aren't much better overall. (Of course, some large and small companies do score A+ in this matter.)

Why Have a Collection Policy?

Not having a clear credit and collection policy is like rowing without a paddle, fighting a war without a battle plan, or conducting a sales campaign without identifying the prospects to contact. In other words, it's ad-libbing, making up the rules as you go along, with everyone having their own, often contradictory, idea of what to do and why.

Every business has a collection policy. *If you don't create one yourself, your customers will do it for you!* Nature abhors a vacuum. It's literally true that every business has a policy. The only question is who determines it, you or your customers.

Another reason for having a policy is that people like to know in advance the rules of the game *before* they play. People don't want surprises. Never tell your customers after you do business what your policy is; do it in *advance*. How'd you like to go to Las Vegas to learn to play craps, put up $10,000 in bets, lose it all, and *then* be told how the betting works? Some companies do business with customers this way. The customers don't know the rules for paying, and when they find out, they say, in effect, "If I'd known that, I wouldn't have bought," which guarantees you collection problems.

Within the same industry, businesses have varying policies, and customers may have been conditioned by your competitors' "easy" payment policy and expect you to acquiesce to the so-called industry standard. If you don't make your rules clear at the outset, the pressure on you and the fear of loss may be more than you can handle.

Still another major reason for having a clearly stated policy is the inherent conflict in many companies between sales and credit. These jobs may be performed by different people or, in a very small business, by one person who wears two hats. Either way, salespeople are motivated to generate sales, even if it means winking at the credit policy a bit or giving the customer more than just the benefit of the doubt. The business office, with responsibility for accounting and profitable sales and without sales' incentives for booking business, is motivated and compensated to enforce whatever credit and collection policies may be in place.

A good example of this potentially inherent business policy conflict is the furniture store salesman who had a young couple come into the store and custom-order a purple, heart-shaped bed. When the bed arrived, the couple took one look at it, were horrified by what they saw, and walked out, leaving the store with an unsalable item. As a result, the store now has a policy that custom-ordered furniture must be paid for in advance, in full.

In summary, here are the five main reasons why you must have a clear credit and collection policy. Without such a clear policy, you'll take on *more nonpaying customers.*

1. If you don't have a policy, your customers will make one for you, and you won't like it.
2. No one likes unpleasant surprises about money. Inform before you perform.
3. Businesses within an industry often have different payment policies. If yours is better than the average or the worst, you'd better spell it out or be dragged down to the most lenient expected norm.
4. Inherent conflicts in how salespeople and credit people are motivated and compensated arise if you don't have a policy that reconciles the two functions.
5. To counter the general fear of loss of business, the policy that's right for your business will allow you to walk away from business that *you* choose to turn your back on, primarily due to the likelihood that you won't get paid.

Why Businesses Avoid Having a Collection Policy

In my consulting work and at seminars, when I ask the audience how many have a good credit and collection policy, fewer than one-third of the hands are raised. The rest of the people readily, almost eagerly, admit that they need to work on it and that it's worth doing. They feel guilty but in good company.

What's going on here? If they know they'll only benefit from having a sound credit and collection policy, why haven't they formulated one? One reason is the fear of being stuck in a rigid, inflexible policy that may be inappropriate for some special situation. Bosses often like to give a dispensation to a customer to show that she's a great person to do business with. We'll discuss this problem shortly and how to overcome it by having an unchanging external policy and an internal policy that allows exceptions.

Another reason is the unwillingness of many bosses to resolve the conflict between sales and credit. Some people just don't relish confrontation or decision making.

Finally, creating a credit and collection policy is hard work. It requires working through conflicting policy components and coming up with the ones right for your business. Then you have to develop effective ways of communicating those policies.

Your Written Internal and External Policies

Your external policy is the one that all customers and prospective customers get to see. It spells out precisely how you do business, the terms, and, in many businesses, the consequences for not living up to the terms.

The external policy is in writing, and each customer gets a copy if that business grants credit. If the business is cash and carry, such as a fast-food restaurant, no written policy is necessary, although even these establishments post written notices about the penalties for bad checks (or, in the case of hotels, the consequences of defrauding an innkeeper). In some businesses, it's a good move to have customers sign the policy or a statement of financial responsibility, particularly where experience shows a pattern of collection problems. The act of signing isn't just for legal protection (you don't want to go to court to enforce payment of every bill). More importantly, signing produces *in the debtor's mind* a sense of obligation, which is why most people are skittish about signing anything.

Here's an example of the value of a signature or even an initial. Plumbing companies tend to have collection problems partly because customers resent the high hourly rate and partly because many customers dispute how long a period of time they should have been billed for at that "exorbitant" rate. One plumbing company solved that problem permanently. When the plumber goes out on a job, he has the customer fill in, on a 3 × 5-inch form, the time the plumber arrived; the customer then initials the card. When the plumber leaves, the plumber records the time on the card and the customer again initials the card. When the bill is sent, a copy of that time slip is sent with it. With this system, the objections, and the collection problems, ended for good. No longer are there disputes about how long the plumber was on the job.

The internal policy is in writing also, but only the business personnel, not the customers, get to see it. The internal policy gives guidelines on how much to deviate from the external policy and under what circumstances, whether in granting credit or in enforcing the collection policy.

The internal policy lets you make controlled exceptions. The external policy tells you what you're making exceptions *from*. Otherwise you're simply making up the exceptions as the spirit moves you, with no attempt at consistency, which is frustrating for your staff and presents to the world a picture of rampant confusion.

Your external policy should be stated clearly, without "weasel words." Don't create a good written external policy and then, at the bottom, have such statements as, "If you require special arrangements, see the business manager" or "If you have any problems complying with our terms, we'll be happy to make mutually satisfactory arrangements with you." These statements sound reasonable and are meant to show thoughtfulness in working with customers who have a temporary financial problem. However, their unintended effect is to *encourage* exceptions. People will take the easiest way out. If they think they can get a deal, they'll take advantage of it. Eliminate these reasonable-sounding offers; simply state your policy. Then, if there *is* a problem in paying, your customer will tell you, either by telling you or by not paying, and you'll use your internal policy to handle the situation and make the exception. But please don't invite collection problems. You have enough aggravation with the ones that will slip in even with the best policy.

How to Communicate Your Policy

I realize that there are exceptions to my comments about internal and external policies. For example, answering services seldom see their customers because all business is done on the phone. However, even answering services can confirm the phone arrangements by sending a copy of their policy to each customer and asking her or him to sign and return it. This arrangement reduces misunderstandings and collection problems.

With these exceptions in mind, my comments on communicating your policy are directed at businesses that grant credit and do see the customers face to face. But even if you don't see your customers, the *concept* of this section is useful.

There are three objectives in communicating your policy. You must do it in such a way that your customers will, in most instances,

1. *Understand* the policy (know precisely what it is).
2. *Follow* the policy (pay you the way you want).
3. *Appreciate* your having taken the trouble to let them know, in advance, the rules of the game.

That's a lot to ask in communicating a policy, so how do

you do it? First, have a policy that looks good. Don't type something and run off poor-looking copies. Spend some money here—it's worth it. Have the policy typeset and printed on good quality paper. (I discuss what's in the policy later.)

Give each new customer *his or her own copy* of the policy (I cover reeducating your *present* customers to a new policy before the chapter ends). Say something such as this as you present the policy:

> Like most people, you probably appreciate knowing in advance how we like to do business, because our policy may be different from other companies you've dealt with, and it just wouldn't be fair to you if we didn't talk about that, wouldn't you agree?
>
> Well, we've put our policy in writing, so that we wouldn't overlook anything, and I'd like you to have a copy of it to look over to see if you're comfortable with it.

Notice how this approach looks out for the customer's interests, although you benefit also.

Even though you've written out a policy, provided a copy for each customer, and acknowledged that your policy may be different than what the customer is used to, that's not enough. You also need *feedback*. You want to know what your customer thinks of your policy and whether he plans to comply with it. (Don't *assume* a customer will understand, follow, and appreciate your policy just because you've taken the trouble to communicate it.) Let's discuss three ways of getting feedback, starting with the worst.

1. Ask, "Do you have any questions about our policy?" This is a bit better than saying nothing and hoping the customer understands the policy, but many people have questions but don't ask them, for two reasons:
   a. Some people are ashamed to ask questions because they think theirs is a "stupid" question and no one likes looking stupid, or they think they *should* have known the answer.

    b. Other people are clever enough to know that the answer to their question will cost them more money than if they keep their mouth shut, so they feel it's better not to ask!

2. Better than asking "Do you have any questions?" is this statement: "Many of our new customers, when they read over our policy, had a question about one part or another of it. Which part or parts weren't 100 percent clear to you?" This approach lets the customer know that asking questions is the natural, expected thing to do, so that customer feels "safer" in doing so.

3. If the response to the previous statement is "No, I have no questions. I understand it all," *don't buy that*. If you know from experience that your customers will resist or go unconscious on some aspect(s) of your policy, bring it up *yourself*. Say, "No questions? Fine. I'd like to point out that many of our customers weren't really clear about (whatever it is), and we feel it's only fair to point out our policy on that since it does differ a bit from some other companies like ours.

I make such a big deal about feedback because it's a superb way of *preventing* collection problems. Many companies, even though they see the "theoretical" merit of this kind of communication, try to invalidate it by pointing out practical considerations. The main excuse is that they're so busy already, how could they possibly find the added time to discuss policy with each new customer.

I sympathize with that point, but my answer may surprise you. If you don't have enough time to discuss policy prior to doing business, you'll spend it afterward, and you'll spend more time. The time will be spent trying to collect the accounts receivable that are higher than they need to be. The level of stress will also be higher. Businesses with bloated receivables often tell us that they haven't got the time or money to invest in the prevention steps I'm describing. My response to them is, "Oh, but you can afford to have a few

hundred thousand excess dollars in your unpaid accounts?"
Whether your efforts are directed to prevention or remedial
action, you pay—you just pay a lot less when you prevent.

How to Change Policy for
Established Customers

For an established business that recognizes the need to create
a better, clearer policy, the prospect of reeducating present
customers is a more daunting prospect than introducing new
customers to the rules because old customers are used to the
old, easy policy, and any change tends to be resisted, especially a change to a "tougher" policy for paying.

For example, if you go to a medical specialist you've never
seen before, you may be asked to pay for the visit on the day
of treatment, in full, regardless of whether you have insurance. You won't particularly like this policy, but you've heard
of it at other doctors, so you pay. But suppose your regular
family doctor, who usually waits to bill you until he gets the
portion paid by insurance, suddenly decides that from now
on you pay at least 30 percent of the bill at the time of treatment, and then he'll wait for insurance to pay the rest. You
won't like this approach any better than the policy of the
specialist, which was tougher (*all* on treatment day, not just
30 percent), but the temptation to get uptight and heap a little verbal abuse on your no-longer-so-kindly doctor may be
too much to bear. Your present doctor is afraid you'll accuse
him of being money hungry, or worse, or that you'll threaten
to take your business elsewhere and tell your friends to do
the same.

So how do you minimize this very real, legitimate fear and
reduce the inevitable loss of a few customers? One way is to
send a copy of your new policy to all established customers
with a cover letter explaining that you've changed your policy on the recommendation of your CPA and you want to

make sure all your customers are aware of it. Avoid the temptation to whine about how higher costs or some other problem of yours is the cause of the change. Your customers aren't responsible for your problems and costs. (If you *are* a CPA, then blame your business consultant, or a board of directors.)

Another method is to present customers with the change when they next receive your product or service. Tell them about the new policy, give them a copy of it, discuss the charge, *but be prepared to let them pay you one more time the old way*, if you need to, should they balk. Going through the change in payment policy is like going through the sound barrier. There's turbulence at the moment of impact, but on the other side is smooth flying and the satisfaction of having met the challenge and having won.

What Should Be in Your Policy

Because of all the various types of businesses, there's no way I can cover all the key components of credit and collection policy for them all. What I can do is anticipate the main interests of businesses and their customers regarding payment and then present general policy components. The following policy considerations might apply in your business. Where appropriate, I indicate if the component is internal; otherwise, it's external. These lists aren't exhaustive, only indicative of the points you may have to spell out for your customers. You'll undoubtedly add or subtract from this list.

General Components

1. Where you're located, hours of business, phone and fax numbers to use for different purposes
2. How long you've been in business, qualifications of business or key people, types of business or consumer you serve, your goals, and your delight at being able to

offer your products or services, which are the best, for these reasons

3. Related products or services you do *not* provide and your willingness to help customer find them
4. Why your policy is now in writing, if it wasn't previously.
5. Whether you charge for design or proposal work that others may execute

Credit Components

1. Credit information you require
2. How much credit to grant as a result of the information gained above. (internal)
3. What to do if the customer doesn't give you all the credit information you request. (internal)
4. An acceptable level of unpaid accounts. (If you have *no* receivables, your credit terms are awfully tough and you're losing too much business that could be profitable.)
5. Who makes credit decisions. (Don't let the boss do it; she's a sucker for bending the rules, because bosses usually love to sell.)
6. If a new customer needs a quick shipment, should we do an abbreviated credit check and provide a small supply? (Internal. This is one way of snagging a new customer. Just ask for, say, a bank name and two vendor references, with a full credit check to come later.)

Terms

1. Allowable forms of payment: cash, check, credit card, money order, barter, letter of credit, etc.
2. Discounts for prompt payment.
3. Service charge or interest for late payments. Charge for bad checks.
4. Return policy.

5. What to do if discount is taken but not earned. (internal)
6. Acceptable tolerances for products.
7. Delivery time and who pays for packing, delivery, or any other special cost.
8. Under what conditions, if any, is payment in advance expected.

Collection Policy

1. When statements are sent. Interval between statements. How many statements are sent.
2. When phone calls are made, for what size accounts.
3. What messages are on statements and in phone calls.
4. Based on account size or other criteria (such as credit information, assets, past payment history, sales potential), when does an account get turned over to an outside firm for collection and when do we write it off.
5. Accounts not paid within X days will be placed for collection. This is appropriate for some businesses and is part of the external policy.
6. Under what conditions do we use a small claims court, a collection attorney, a precollection letter service, a collection agency, or a temporary in-house collector? Based on dollar limit, who decides?
7. If customer doesn't pay as agreed but makes some attempt to pay, how far to negotiate? *Example*: Is it OK to accept an offer of a $10 payment on a $200 account?
8. Notice needed to terminate contract. Penalties, if any.

How to Create Or Change Your Policy

Once you decide that it would be a good idea to put together a credit and collection policy or to change the present one, how do you go about it? After all, your collection policy is a big part of your business strategy, and you don't approach it casually. Following are useful suggestions.

1. The boss must be involved, along with the key department heads, every step of the way.

2. Begin by stating your intention to create or revamp your credit and collection policy and the reasons for doing so. Name the people who'll be involved in the process.

3. Have the first meeting.

    a. Discuss the problems that present policy is creating.

    b. Develop a list of components that a policy is needed to address.

    c. Ask everyone to spend the next week or two writing down their version of a policy for dealing with these components.

4. Have a second meeting and resolve the ideas.

5. Get outside help if you need it. Get sample policies from others. Let everyone read this book. Above all, get started.

I can almost guarantee that your present policy doesn't serve your interests as well as it should. Worse, it doesn't serve your customers as well as they deserve. People and businesses will pay, even a premium, if they get quality, service, reliability, and courtesy *and* if they know in advance all about the rules of doing business with you.

Conclusion: Get wisdom and understanding, but above all get a policy.

7

Granting Credit—and Not Granting Credit

Credit granting is an art and a science. The scientific part is represented by the historical data built up over many years. For example, of ten new customers, you can expect two to four to be one-time sales and a small credit loss. Six to eight will become valuable customers, with two paying within sixty to ninety days.

Information Needed

Before granting credit to a new commercial customer, you should obtain the following basic information (unless it's a large public company):

1. Whether the customer is an individual, a partnership, or a corporation. You need names and addresses of all owners, partners, or officers.
2. How long the company has been in business (50 percent of business failures are companies less than one year old; 75 percent less than five years old).

3. Bank name and address, average bank balance, any loans outstanding.
4. Financial statement. This is a must. Reluctance to provide it is a clue to eventual collection problems.
5. Three businesses the applicant is now doing business with and the bill-paying history with them.

For consumer debt, you want as much information as possible, consistent with the size of the bill, whether or not the customer is one-time or ongoing, and many other factors specific to certain business. The basic information you want is:

1. Name of person responsible, along with that person's address, spouse, home phone number. Sometimes you'll add driver's license number and social security number.
2. Place of employment for both spouses: name, address, how long there, phone number. This information doubles the chances of collecting.
3. Type of employment. This is a major tipoff as to collectability. For example, self-employed sometimes means unemployed; certain occupations are notoriously unstable.
4. Bank reference.
5. Personal references.
6. Whether consumer rents, leases, or owns, and for how long.
7. Former addresses.

Many credit applications are considerably nosier than these questions, but the more information you have, the better. Your ability to skiptrace (see Chapter 21) is directly related to how much information you have.

The credit information on your consumer customers becomes obsolete rapidly. In this country, which is a mobile society, some key information about your consumer debtors changes every five years, for example, where they live or where they're employed. That means that 20 percent of the data in your customer files becomes useless each year! No wonder you get skips. In fact, 30 percent of all accounts that go to collection agencies wind up there because you can no longer find the debtor, which is why a simple way to cut down on skips is to update your regular customers' files every year or two. Ask them, "Where are you living now?" and "Where are you working now?" Notice I did *not* say "Are you still living at ———?" It's too easy for the consumers to say "Yes"; you want them to either confirm or correct the information.

Suppose your consumer debtor is reluctant to give you all the information you request, whether from laziness or from a need to hide something. This reluctance could signal collection problems later. Here are three approaches to this common problem:

1. Ask the consumer to fill in the missing information or you ask the questions and complete the form yourself.

2. Show understanding of the customer's reasons for resistance. Say, "You know, filling out credit applications is a first-rate pain in the neck. Everywhere you go, they ask for the same information, over and over. You'd think they'd have a big computer somewhere that shares all the information, and I think people should know just by looking at me that I'm honest. So, I understand. But, if you would take just a minute more, we really do need this additional information." If your debtor continues to fight after you've showed so much compassion for legitimate-sounding reasons for withholding information, you can expect that the remaining reasons will result in you not getting paid.

3. If the debtor absolutely refuses to give key credit information, then you can do business on a cash or COD basis—no credit. Be prepared to walk away from such risky business.

Many businesses provide a product or service for which it makes sense to have the customer sign a document that defines how payment will be made and any penalties for nonperformance, including court costs and attorney fees. I'm not suggesting that you need this for all types of business. What I am saying is that even the best credit granting information you can get still leaves you hoping the debtor will pay, but hope may not be good enough. A little more certainty, in the form of signed and enforceable (and believable) legal papers, is good security in many business transactions.

Role of the Credit Department

According to Tom Gorman of the *New York Times*, others in companies have long viewed the credit department as little more than a bill collector. But, growing in complexity and sophistication, the credit department is slowly shedding its green eyeshade image and gaining respectability. "Over the last five years, companies have come to realize that accounts receivable are one of the biggest assets on their books," said Robert A. Johnston, president of the National Association of Credit Management. As a result, companies are beginning to view their accounts receivable as credit portfolios that are to be managed. Some credit managers now assess the quality of those accounts rather than simply track their incoming flow. And they earn higher salaries to do so. About 8 percent of the association's 40,000 members make "six figures," Johnston said.

The increased risk of extending credit has also elevated the role of the credit department. In 1988, 57,000 companies with outstanding credit of $36 billion went under, up alarmingly from 6600 failures in 1978, according to Dun & Bradstreet Corporation.Even worse, declaring bankruptcy has become an acceptable business practice rather than a last resort strategy.

As the risks rise, more companies are moving toward insuring their accounts receivables, as 5 percent of U.S. companies are doing. In Europe, where there are no credit-reporting services comparable to Dun & Bradstreet, about 50 percent of the companies carry some form of receivables insurance. In the United States, this insurance has been growing fast. In 1988, $88 million was spent on premiums. The main insurers today are American Credit Indemnity, now a division of Dun & Bradstreet, and Continental Guaranty.

In addition to growing credit risks, another reason for the growth in receivables insurance is a change caused by the 1986 tax code. To cover their credit losses, large companies traditionally have set aside bad debt reserves equal to less than 1 percent of gross revenues. All these reserves can no longer be deducted from their taxes, and by 1991, none of the reserves will be deductible. The insurance, however, is fully deductible and allows companies to put cash in reserves to better use.

The credit department is also rapidly becoming automated. According to the Pertacon, Inc. 1988 survey of 370 companies, 46 percent of companies with less than $100 million in sales had personal computers in their credit department, compared to only 19 percent in 1985.

Charles Bodenstab, in an article in *Inc.* magazine,* prepared a marvelously tongue-in-cheek approach on how *not* to handle credit:

1. Start with an unknown individual who has a minimum of capital and a great story about his prospects in a far corner of the state.

2. Offer extended terms so he can finance the inventory needed to generate the fantastic business he has described.

3. When he is past due on his payments, rationalize that this is temporary, perhaps because of seasonality.

4. Let the account's salesperson verify that the inventory is in fact in place.

---

*Reprinted with permission, *Inc.* magazine, (May, 1989). Copyright © 1989 by Goldhirsh Group, Inc., 38 Commercial Wharf, Boston, MA 02110.

5. As you look at the financial statements, be sympathetic that this is a new operation having trouble getting a handle on its operating results.

6. When you start to realize your customer is in trouble, don't take your losses early. Stick with him, and you ought to be able to double the account you have to write off.

Bodenstab developed a procedure for monitoring 3000 accounts without personally having to (or anybody else having to) wade through a mind-numbing computer printout of data. He created a month-end exception reporting system that isolates two groups of accounts:

1. Accounts that have undergone a statistically significant adverse change. This is seldom more than 80 accounts out of the 3000 total, but they make up 99 percent of the short-term problems.

2. Accounts with a history of problems, which need to be monitored. This again is about 100 accounts out of 3000 but covers 99 percent of the chronic offenders.

Although a business needs to protect itself from unnecessary credit loss, it can be too protective. Company policy must include a measure of acceptable loss because growth can be achieved only by taking reasonable risk. Reserves for bad debts and collection costs are an acceptable, recognized expense for business. They go with the territory. However, if you grant credit, it should be mostly at your option, not involuntary philanthropy.

Conclusion: Credit is a business tool. Don't be overly concerned about whether or not you have the perfect credit application. Focus instead on having a clearly stated, specific credit policy, policy goals, and a credit system. Be sure your salespeople live it as completely as your credit manager does.

8

Seven Payment Strategies That Work

N ow let's get specific about how you'll let customers pay you. We've seen that your payment policy consists of two sections: the external policy and the internal one. The external policy is clear, unambiguous, in writing, and presented to each customer whenever possible. In some businesses, the customer must sign a related document of financial responsibility. The internal policy spells out what to do when customers don't abide by the external policy.

In this chapter, you'll learn the most commonly used payment options and how to implement them. In each case, I've labeled the option as part of either the internal or the external policy.

Payment in Full Now With Cash, Check, Discount, or Charge Card (External)

This payment option is obviously the best for your business. If everyone paid this way, there'd be no need for this book. To encourage more payments in full, businesses have devised various strategies for encouraging customers to pay in full, or at least to pay sooner.

Payment by Cash

This method is impractical for some customers and impossible for large purchases, but from your point of view it's the safest, cheapest form of payment. Go for it.

Payment by Check

A check may be as good as cash, although there's a delay before the money is credited to your account. Unlike cash, a check can be bad, so there's some risk in accepting a check. For a fee, check protection companies will guarantee checks above a certain amount. You have to compare the cost of the service with the savings in bad checks you'll avoid. The leading nationwide check guarantee companies are Checkrite and Telecheck.

Discounts or Prizes for Payment Now

A common practice is to give a discount or a premium to encourage customers to pay more money *now*. As we've seen, *everyone loves a bargain*, no matter how much money they have. We've also seen that paying bills is a matter of priority. Most people and businesses have more bills and a longer wish list than money to pay for them. Accordingly, you want to make it easier for your customer to send money your way instead of to someone else. A bargain in the form of a discount or free gift is a good solution.

Some people become a bit short-sighted about this concept. They ask, "Why should I give a discount for payment today when I'm going to get paid by a lot of people today anyway?" The answer is that you'll get paid *more* today with a discount. The problem of the shortsighted is that they look at what they're giving up—the 2 to 10 percent discount.

They fail to see what they're gaining in greater net dollars. This myopic view is also held by those credit grantors who hesitate to offer payment by charge card because they have to pay the bank up to 5 percent for the service. They fail to notice that the charge card method has two powerful benefits:

1. You get your money. If you don't get it now, you may not get it at all.
2. Money paid now earns interest income.

The combined effects of these benefits usually exceed the "loss" from the bank charge. In other words, you're playing the percentages shrewdly by offering charge card payment or a discount.

One more thought on discounts. Many businesses have a discount policy something like this: 5 percent if paid on receipt of invoice, 2 percent if paid within thirty days. Such a policy is productive because it puts a price on paying promptly.

Payment by Charge Card

This option is used mostly for consumer businesses because the dollar limit MasterCard, Visa, Amex and others impose makes it impractical for businesses with large purchases, although airline affinity cards are being used for business purchases at an increasing rate. Some businesses, particularly doctors, hospitals, accountants, lawyers, and other professionals, avoid offering payment by charge card, not just for the so-called economic loss previously described but because they feel that it's somehow tacky for their profession and that some of their clients may accuse them of unprofessionalism.

Here's how to look at this conflict and how to handle it. First, recognize that most people and businesses have charge cards and use them regularly, even eagerly. Why? Simple:

The cards cut down the need to carry cash, and they delay the need to pay the charge card bill for thirty days, at no interest. So, doctors, lawyers, and other businesspeople, you're doing your patients and clients a favor when you let them pay the way most of them like to pay anyway—with a charge card.

As to the occasional clients who look down their noses and say your charge card system is lowering your professional standards, respond with, "You know, several of our other clients said the same thing, and I really appreciate your stating your views so clearly. That's why we waited so long to put this into effect, because we didn't want to offend valued clients like you. But I must be candid with you. So many of our *other* clients have been asking us, for years, if they could please pay us the way they like to pay their other bills—with a credit card. Naturally, we felt it was only fair to accommodate their wishes. We will, of course, continue to work with you as we always have, and your check is always welcome."

If you accept payment by charge, I suggest you take MasterCard, Visa, and American Express; these cards will handle most of your charge card business. Getting into the charge program is simple: Call up your bank and/or American Express; they'll come to your office with all the necessary materials and train you in the use of them.

Payments (Internal)

Suppose you've tried all the strategies for getting payment in full and they've all bombed. One of your internal options is to offer payments. Notice I said "internal." Recall from Chapter 6 that your external policy is silent about what you may offer a customer who won't pay the way you specify. And you definitely don't include wording such as this on your external policy: "In special circumstances, payments will be offered" or "Please see our Business Manager if you are unable to pay the full amount." Would any business issue such an invitation to delay payment? More than would admit it!

You have a limited number of payment offers to make if you can't get payment in full. The first is two payments. The next, obviously, is three. When you make these offers, you must make it clear that you're breaking the rules, this is a one-time offer only—no precedent is being set—and you may even risk getting into trouble by offering the option. At the very least, you may generate some goodwill or gratitude for being willing to break the rules for your customer. The debtor will feel that he or she is special.

When you go to four or more payments, a wonderful tool available to you is called Regulation Z of the Federal Truth-in-Lending Act. Regulation Z states that if you and the debtor agree to four or more payments, this provision falls under the regulation and you *may* then have the debtor fill out *and sign* a Truth-in-Lending Disclosure Form (sold at law supply firms or stationery stores).

Before I tell you how to use Regulation Z, let me clarify the implications of the rules. Regulation Z applies if you and a customer agree to four or more payments. If the customer just sends in four or more payments on his own, without your prior agreement, Regulation Z doesn't fit. Notice I said that you *may* have the customer fill out and sign the disclosure form. I didn't say you *must* do it; at times you may not want to be bothered. The FTC won't throw you into jail for not bothering. One more point. You can use Regulation Z whether or not you use interest.

When the customer wants to make four or more payments, fill in the blanks on the form and have the customer sign the form. You now have a signed promissory note that has weight in court if you have to sue. Even better, in the customer's mind, he has made a commitment to pay, increasing the probability of payment. If he doesn't sign, you tell him that he may pay in three or fewer payments. Either way, you come out ahead.

Envelope and Stamp (Internal)

This technique is popular with doctors, lawyers, and other businesses that have face-to-face contact with customers who like to be billed. When asked to be billed, the business manager says, "We'd be happy to bill you. But the best way to handle this is for you to take this envelope and statement with you, write out a check when you get home, and send it in. That way you'll have one less bill to worry about." Some people will take the envelope, others won't. Those who do and who pay result in that much less billing. When you're playing the percentages, every technique counts.

A nice touch with this technique, after you've presented the envelope and statement, is to add, as though it were an afterthought, "Oh, let me put a stamp on that for you." Then you offer two or three different stamps and let the customer choose one. People like to make choices. One business manager I know even gets her stamps out of her purse. Talk about inflicting guilt and obligation on the debtor!

To justify this technique, don't tell a customer that you are trying to cut costs and avoid raising prices. That's an acceptable point of view, but the technique works better if your attitude suggests that offering the envelope is a good way of serving the customer.

Postdated Checks (Internal)

Let's begin this discussion by recognizing that some people don't believe that it is legal to take a postdated check. (This is a check dated in the future, typically on paydays.) In a *few* states, that's true. With those exceptions, it's perfectly OK to ask for postdated checks. What you may *not* do is deposit the check prior to the date on the check.

Call or write the customer at least three days prior to the date on the check and state that you're going to put the check through. Note that you didn't ask if you could put it through; you took an assumptive approach and said you were planning to do it. The debtor can still tell you not to do it because of lack of funds, in which case you don't put that check through and you discuss how the debtor plans to handle this latest development.

To use this technique, when your customer offers a partial payment, accept that payment and immediately ask for the balance in the form of a postdated check or checks. Present this option as a service to customers, indicating that now the burden is on you to call the customer prior to each deposit date and to handle all the paperwork. By giving you the checks, in other words, the customer's obligation is finished.

If you get your check(s), your bill is practically paid in full with minimal cost and time otherwise spent in multiple billings or phone calls. However, if a customer balks at giving you the postdated checks, you still come out ahead because you now have strong evidence of a debtor who's unwilling to accept payment options that make life easy. You can find out early who's likely to become a collection problem and act accordingly. There's no point in giving a lot of rope to someone who'll hang you with it.

Other Sources of Money (Internal)

If a debtor tells you she doesn't have any money or not enough money, you're approaching a minefield. Part of the problem is the debtor's implication or statement that she has other bills to pay and yours can wait. You're in a serious negotiation and you need several kinds of ammunition. You need to know the many places that debtors can go to get money—I list them later in the chapter.

What's tough is knowing the techniques to use to convince your debtor to seek out money from those sources. Debtors often do not want to be bothered getting money for you, or they act as if it's none of your business how they'll pay you.

Although you shouldn't get self-righteous about it, you have every right to ask for credit information and specifics about how the debtor will pay you.

First, let's deal with a trap. When a debtor tells you she just can't pay you in full or has no money, obviously she has other bills and feels that many of them take priority over yours. You may not like that fact, but it's true. So your best negotiating strategy is to acknowledge reality. Say something like, "Obviously, Ms. Debtor, if you can't pay us, it's because you have other bills to pay and I'll bet some of those folks are hounding you for money. Isn't that so? Well, we don't want to be that kind of company. We want to work this out with you, if that's OK with you." Ask for agreement, then say, "If there were somehow, somewhere a source of money to take care of this bill and maybe some of the other ones you have, and take this aggravation off your shoulders, would you like to know about it?" The answer will be yes, no, or a suspicious maybe. If it's no, you know you have a Grade A collection problem, so don't waste time before turning the account over to some third party if the debtor won't cooperate.

If the answer is maybe, just point out that you deal with this kind of situation all the time and you know you can be helpful. You'll eventually get a yes or a no. If the answer is yes, you've got her! She has now given you permission to do credit counseling. She has said, in effect, tell me how and where I can get the money to pay you. Now you list all the ways money can be obtained.

1. Loan from a bank
2. Loan from a credit union
3. Loan from a finance company
4. Personal loan from relatives or friends
5. Rewrite existing loan for higher amount
6. Borrow on whole life insurance at 5 percent interest
7. Salary advance
8. Second job

9. Sell stocks
10. Loan with a cosigner
11. Second mortgage on property
12. MasterCard, Visa
13. Coins, jewelry, paintings
14. Personal service or barter in exchange for your products or service
15. Consumer Credit Counselors, a nonprofit organization that in most communities will assist debtors in managing money and work with all credit grantors in an impartial manner.

Do some of these sources of money seem preposterous? Maybe, but many debtors aren't aware of them or won't consider using them to pay you without your prompting.

Refusal to Accept Initial Offer (Internal)

Whenever a debtor offers to pay less than the full amount, you must refuse to accept it because the debtor's first offer is never the best one. *It's the worst one*. The debtor wants to spread the money around, and you need some negotiating strategy. You refuse, graciously but firmly, by saying, "I wish I could accept that, but our company won't allow it." At this point, the debtor may say, "Well, that's all I have" or "What would you accept?" If he gives the former reply, repeat that you just can't accept it and, if forced into it, you point out what you'd have to do if he won't cooperate.

If the debtor asks, "What would you accept?", *never* name a figure other than about three-fourths of the full amount now and the balance with a postdated check. If this offer is refused, continue to liberalize the terms—and let the debtor struggle with you—until you feel you've gotten as much as you can.

Don't hesitate to say no to any offer that's ridiculous or

vague. You can always go back and make a deal later. You simply don't want to give away too much too soon. When you do accept, do so with the understanding that you're bending over backward and that the debtor had better not welch on the deal.

Amnesty (Internal)

This technique is used to clear up old unpaid bills. Government agencies do it to get parking tickets cleared up or, in a variation, to get unauthorized weapons turned in, no questions asked.

There are three elements to an amnesty:

1. Age of the bills to which the amnesty will apply
2. Deal offered if those bills are paid
3. Time given the debtors to accept the amnesty before it expires

Here's an example how amnesty works: For all bills six months or older, you'll give a 20 percent discount and consider it paid in full if it's paid within thirty days. You send this notice to all debtors whose bills qualify. You make it clear that this is a one-time offer only. You'll find that a gratifying amount of money will flow in. Did you lose 20 percent of your money by the offer? Not really, because the likelihood of collecting on accounts older than six months is much less than 80 percent—more like 20 to 50 percent. So if you collect 80 percent of the bills paid under the amnesty you're way ahead. As for those debtors who don't respond to the amnesty, you have real problems and should quickly assign them to a third-party agency for collection.

Finally, let's look at all seven payment strategies from the standpoint of priority. That is, which strategies should you use first to increase the odds of getting more money sooner?

The other strategies will produce less money but are the best to use under increasingly difficult circumstances.

1. Ask for all the money now.
2. Ask for part of the money now and the balance with a post-dated check(s). All the money is now in your hands, although it can't be deposited in your bank.
3. Give an envelope and stamp and ask for the balance in full.
4. If you can't get payment in full through strategies 1 to 3, refuse to accept any initial offer the debtor presents.
5. When you're forced into accepting payments, go for two; back down slowly to more than two when you must.
6. Know sources of money and how to sell the debtor on seeking some of them when the debtor claims little or no ability to pay.
7. For accounts that have been allowed to get too old, offer an amnesty to clear the decks and present a fresh start.

Conclusion: Your repertoire for getting debtors to pay you should now be as large and creative as the excuses many debtors invent so they can hang onto your money as long as possible.

9

Drawing the Line— Somebody's Got to Do It

Most of us tend to oversimplify. Matters are either black or white, good or bad. People are type A or type B, sensitive or callous, open or secretive. However, reality is more often shades of gray. Many times I've heard collectors say that a debtor either will or won't pay. That's true as far as it goes. Depending on how much time and effort you put into collecting an account, debtors either will or won't pay, but they may also just pay a portion and then stop paying. Therefore, the pay/not pay dichotomy isn't a useful model to use in deciding how much effort to put into collecting an account.

The model I prefer is called the Spectrum of Debtors. This model is not only a look at people as they really are, it's also a practical tool for enabling a collector to make the most realistic judgment about whether a debtor is going to pay or not, to decide how much added effort to put into collecting, and to determine the likelihood of success. These benefits aren't certainties; they're just the best possible odds you can expect in this unpredictable world.

The Spectrum of Debtors

Below is an illustration of the Spectrum of Debtors.

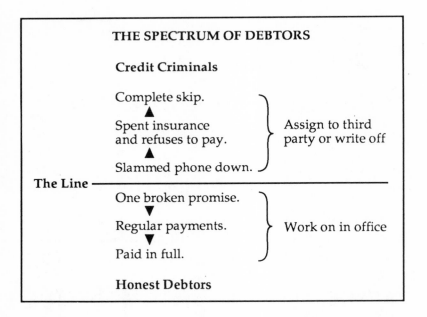

I urge you to make a copy of it and put the copy by the phone of anyone in your company who does collecting. Now let's analyze the spectrum.

A spectrum is a continuum, such as the colors of a rainbow, which go from violet to red, or radio or television frequencies, which you can pick up by moving the dial. Debtors also come in a spectrum. It isn't true that they'll either pay or not pay; that depends on how much urgency you create, how many other bills or spending fantasies your debtor has, and how much time you can afford to put in collecting any one account. Anyone can justify not paying a bill, not paying all the bill, or delaying payment with good reason, such as poor service, or apparent misrepresentation by the seller. Thus, if an individual can be either an honest debtor or a less than honest one, it follows that a group of people will be found all over the debtor spectrum.

In our spectrum, at one end are the *honest debtors*, who pay their debts immediately, in full, with no aggravation. Most debtors are honest, but not all are—if they were, you wouldn't be reading this book. At the other end of the spectrum are what collection professionals call *credit criminals*. These people lie, give false credit information, skip town, promise you anything, and deliver nothing. They're the con artists of the world, taking advantage of their victims' trusting natures. Some of the best are good looking, well-dressed, and articulate, and they can look you right in the eye while they make totally false promises. A credit criminal can sell you worthless gold mines, cattle ranches, or the Brooklyn Bridge. This person can cost you your life savings.

Thus we have the honest people at one end of the spectrum, the credit criminals at the other end, and all the other people in between. Before we're finished, we'll want to know where on the spectrum to place a debtor when you've completed a communication with him because your future actions will depend on that placement. The spectrum is a *decision tool*.

In the middle of the spectrum is *the line*. I refer to debtors as above-the-line debtors or below-the-line debtors. In a minute, we'll see how to place debtors on the spectrum. For now, remember that if a debtor winds up above the line, you should stop work on the account and write it off, take it to a small-claims court, give it to a collection attorney, or assign it to a collection service. If the debtor is placed below the line, continue to work on that account in your office, at least one more time. When you're just not sure where to put the debtor, put her on the line. If I'm not sure, I'm willing to put the debtor on the line *once*. My philosophy includes giving the benefit of the doubt *one time*. I'll accept one broken promise, not two.

Above-the-Line Debtors

Representative examples of above-the-line actions, beginning with the worst credit criminals and moving toward the
line (not necessarily in perfect order) are

1. Pays with stolen credit card
2. Refuses to pay
3. Writes a worthless check
4. Skips town
5. Gives phony credit information
6. Never returns phone calls
7. Slams down phone
8. Curses or screams at you
9. Got the insurance check and denies receiving it
10. Files bankruptcy
11. Has "other bills to pay"
12. Sends partial payment on a check marked "Paid in Full"
13. Endless excuses

Let's continue at the line with some debtor actions and move
toward the honest debtor:

1. Sends check to the wrong address
2. Says "Never got the bill" but address is correct
3. Says "I can't pay you till they pay me"
4. One broken promise
5. Says "Spouse handles bills"
6. Makes partial payment smaller than agreed
7. Can't speak English
8. One reasonable sounding excuse
9. Ignores one statement
10. Will pay half now and balance in two weeks

11. Accepts return envelope and invoice and promises to pay as soon as she gets home

12. Apologizes for overlooking—will pay immediately

In addition to placing individuals on the spectrum, we can also, unfortunately, place certain groups of people above the line. I say unfortunately because many individuals within a group are responsible, but we can't ignore the evidence about group nature accumulated over the years. Groups who tend to pay above the line include college students, transients, people who live in certain parts of town, people with no credit cards, and street people. Of course, in each group there are highly responsible people; here we're generalizing.

Earlier in the book, I compared collecting with selling. One key point of the comparison was the need to qualify the prospect because the salesperson can't justify spending equal time with all prospects and the collector can't spend the same amount of time with each debtor. The collector makes judgments about how much time to spend on an account by considering the

1. Size of the account in dollars
2. Age of the account
3. Previous payment history
4. Existing credit information on the account
5. Amount of *other* accounts to be worked
6. Other factors
7. *Likelihood that collector intervention will pay off*

The professional collector must ask a fundamental question at the end of each collection activity: "As a result of what the debtor said or did (or didn't do), is my debtor above the line, below it, or on the line?" In my experience with individuals and groups, the collector almost always knows, regardless of how little experience she or he has! Naturally, more experienced collectors are better judges of whether or not a debtor is trying to pull the wool over their eyes, but even beginners have an instinctive awareness—an ability to listen with the inner ear—and hear what the debtor is *really* saying as compared to the words spoken. This phenomenon, which is a right-brain, or intuitive, function, allows the collector to minimize the time spent kidding himself that a debtor will do something positive when the "vibes" are negative or the previous evidence just doesn't support one more excuse.

Not only does the spectrum encourage decisions that have the best odds of being correct, it gives collectors, and management, the freedom to make those decisions at the right time rather than allowing some arbitrary delay. For example, a company's general policy may be to work on accounts above $200 for five months before turning them over to a collection agency. But if an account proves to be a complete skip two weeks after the first bill is sent, that account is clearly above the line and needs to be turned over to the agency right now. Nothing is gained by holding it. In fact, a great deal is lost by waiting. Particularly with skips, the trail gets cold fast.

In Chapter 14, I explain the time value of money and its impact on making informed decisions about how extensively to work on an account and when to give up. Because businesses almost always hang on to unpaid accounts too long, with devastating cash flow results, the Spectrum of Debtors is an essential tool in the management of unpaid accounts.

In summary, the spectrum lets you

1. See people as they really are, not as you might like them to be.
2. Decide how much additional time and money to invest in each account.
3. Communicate in a common language with management about the status of accounts.
4. Bite the bullet more quickly on nonperforming accounts.

5. Train new collectors more quickly.

(Role playing, discussed in Chapter 16, is also used for the training.)

———————

Conclusion: People are wonderful, but some less wonderful than others.

10

Billing and Collecting:
Step by Step

Here's a diagram of a billing and collecting system:

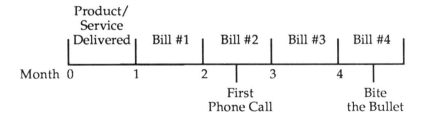

In this chapter, I analyze each step of the system; in Chapters 11 through 14, I examine the key components of the system even further. But first you've got to have a system and a purpose for it. The purpose is to collect as many unpaid accounts as quickly as possible, with as little investment of time and money as possible, and with the least possible loss of business. The system I present shows a resolution of all accounts within four and one-half months (this can be expanded to two or more systems).

Hospitals, for example, usually have two systems: inpatient and outpatient. The inpatient accounts are the largest, have the most credit information, are fewer in number, and therefore get worked an average of four to six months. The outpatient and emergency room accounts have a much smaller dollar value, provide the least credit information, occur in much greater volume, and therefore usually get resolved in two to three months in the well-managed hospital.

As I see it, the professional billing and collecting system begins with two preliminary steps, both of which I've written about in earlier chapters and which are now positioned in their proper place in the system. Let's briefly reiterate these steps and then discuss what's necessary for completing the system.

Step 1: Your Billing and Collection Policy

You already know all about the value of this policy. This is the starting point of the system. Without a well thought-out policy, the rest of the system is built on sand.

Step 2: Gather Credit Information

Unless you are in a cash-and-carry business, the more you know about your customer's payment habits, the better off you are.

Step 3: Deliver Product or Service

Although there's nothing wrong about getting paid in advance before delivering your product or service, as many businesses do, such as hotels and airlines, the typical business gets paid *at* or after the time of purchase. If payment in full isn't made at that time, a bill is delivered, and the business hopes for payment before the next billing period.

So far, there isn't much collection work going on, other than asking for payment at the time of delivery, so the need to do any billing is minimized or eliminated. In Chapter 8, which discussed seven payment strategies, I listed several alternatives to increase the amount you get paid so as to cut back the need to send bills and make collection phone calls. But as you know, you can't completely eliminate the steps that may be necessary for further pursuing payment.

Step 4: Statement 1

Statement (or bill) 1 is sent whenever in the month bills are sent. This statement is "gentle," more of a reminder than a demand for payment. But even the reminder must serve the objective of creating *urgency* about paying the bill. Statement 1 should contain the following elements:

1. Legibility.
2. Notice saying when money is due. Stating the amount due isn't as effective as adding that it is due *now*, or within seven days, or whenever you decide you want it. Remember, if you ask, you're more likely to get.
3. Itemization of purchases if more than one thing is purchased. A customer who made several purchases at one time tends to forget the details when the bill arrives. Therefore, a bill for six items that says "Merchandise— $479.25" isn't nearly as helpful as a bill that spells out each item, its cost, and the total amount owed.
4. Return envelope. Prepaid postage usually isn't necessary.
5. Various options:
   a. Thank the customer for the business.
   b. State how much interest, if any, is charged, and when.
   c. In a business with a high risk of delinquent accounts,

state that unpaid accounts are turned over to a collection agency or a credit reporting company. (Implication: Don't mess around; pay now.)

d. Enclose a sales flyer.

e. Enclose a survey or referral request—how do you like your new item.

Step 5: Statement 2

Most businesses send statement 2 one month after statement 1, *but you don't have to wait that long.* If you bill twice a month, usually you'll get considerably more money than what you spend vs. billing only once a month. The several issues to consider in billing more frequently than once a month are:

1. Billing is "normally" done once a month because that's how it has been done for a long time. But there's no requirement, legal or otherwise, that limits the interval between bills (other than harassment statutes that would discourage billing every other day, to cite a ridiculous example). I suspect that the one-month billing interval was established prior to the advent of computers, when creating and sending bills was a big production, and a one-month interval was considered a reasonable compromise between the effort of doing the billing and the penalty for allowing a longer interval.

2. Whether or not you are cycle billing, in which different letters of the alphabet are billed at different times of the month. A cycle billing system spreads the billing process out over the entire month instead of having it occur all at one time. The bills for debtors whose last names begin with A through F may go out the first third of the month; G through R, the second third; and S through Z the final third. With cycle billing you can still bill each cycle twice a month instead of once.

3. If you change from once a month to twice a month billing, many established customers will notice the change and may even resist the pressure. That's OK. We're still playing the percentages; for the few customers who balk, far more will pay quicker. Companies who shorten the intervals between bills invariably report that the change produced a significant improvement in payments.

4. If, for some reason, you don't want to make an across-the-board change in your billing frequency, please consider increasing the frequency for at least these two types of account:

   a. *Big bills.* Whatever you define as big bills in your business, I'd certainly want you to give more than the average level of attention to seeing that those accounts get paid.

   b. *Older bills.* If you bill once a month in the early stages, and you insist on hanging on to unpaid accounts for, say, nine or ten months, would you please consider billing twice a month for all accounts five to nine months old?

The collection message you put on statement 2 should be gentle. Appropriate messages are "Please," "Past Due," and "Entire Amount Now Due." These messages can be computer printed, typed, or, if volume permits, handwritten (there's more information on written communications in the next chapter). Some companies put stickers with stronger and stronger messages on their statements. These stickers are OK, but I'm biased against them, based on the overall experience of companies who use them.It seems that the customers ignore the yellow and green stickers, waiting for the red one, which shows them that now you're *really* serious.

Computers play a bigger role in generating statements, and some companies use a computer service that sends out the bills directly—the client company doesn't see the bills and can't make any customized collection notations on them.

Given that restriction, use as many of these billing techniques as you can, and ask the billing service to serve your needs. If they can't, look elsewhere.

Step 6: First Phone Call

Phone calls are terribly important (Chapter 12 is a complete discussion of the subject). The most brilliantly written statement doesn't remotely approach the effectiveness of a reasonably well-done collection phone call. A phone call is five to ten times more productive than sending out a bill (trust me), but you can't make a phone call the first collection step because the volume would bury you and it's cheaper to have your first collection communication be written statement 1. However, the phone call is quickest in getting the debtor feedback that will resolve the account.

Many people feel uncomfortable in making collection phone calls and hate the embarrassment of rejection when the debtor responds in a nasty way. In fact, most people who do collection work in a business admit that they don't make nearly as many phone calls as they should. Before we're finished, I hope to have you readers who are collectors not only unafraid of debtor resistance but actually glad to get it, because you'll know exactly how to handle it and also because you know the sooner you confront the resistance, the better off you'll be.

Step 6 is the *first* phone call. Many accounts will require further phone calls later in the system. I won't make any special mention of them or create additional steps on the billing and collecting system. The circumstances of each account and your use of the Spectrum of Debtors will guide you as to how many additional phone calls are needed.

If you're "too busy" to make the phone calls you need, either hire a collector temporary or, if your volume justifies such action, a permanent collector. Phone collectors will pay for themselves easily.

The explosive growth of telemarketing is further tribute to the power of the phone in obtaining appointments and making sales. With telemarketing companies generating so many trained phone people, including students and housewives, your business is probably surrounded by a growing pool of people who are good on the phone, nearby, available for work on a part-time basis, and inexpensive.

Make the phone call ten days to two weeks after statement 2 has been mailed; this is plenty of time for the bill to go out and for the debtor to call you about it. Two weeks is also sufficient for the bill to go out and the debtor to return the money to you. If that doesn't happen in two weeks, or even ten days, I see no point in waiting another two weeks for statement 3. The exceptions are large companies that have a pattern of taking longer than two weeks to respond to statements.

Step 7: Statement 3

Statement 3 isn't the gentle reminder that statement 2 was. In statement 3, you want to tell your debtor, in no uncertain terms, that the bill must now be paid in full.

For example, "This account must be taken care of now," or "We don't understand why this hasn't been paid. Will you please send the balance today. Thank you." Statement 3 doesn't say what you're going to do if the debtor doesn't pay as requested—that is described in statement 4. Also, statement 3 contains no messages such as, "There must be some good reason why we haven't heard from you." All debtors can come up with a reason for delaying payment, so don't encourage them. Statement 3 says what you want (payment in full), when you want it (now), and allows no request for an excuse and doesn't spell out consequences for not paying.

As you can see, the components of the billing and collecting system are all conceived purposefully, not haphazardly, letting you resolve accounts in four months instead of nine or ten. But if phone calls are so great, why would we even be dealing with statement 3 or 4? There are three good reasons for these actions:

1. Some debtors, particularly consumers as compared to other businesses, don't have a phone, don't answer the phone, won't respond to a recorded call, or have an unlisted number.
2. Some phone calls are unproductive. You get no commitment and accomplish nothing, so you have to continue the communication in writing.
3. Sometimes you do reach the debtor on the phone and you do get an agreement to pay in full. Even so, it's a good idea to confirm in writing what the debtor agreed to verbally.

Step 8: Statement 4

Unless the account has already been paid in full, or you and your debtor have agreed on a payment plan for several more payments, this is the last statement. Statement 4 says what you'll do and when you'll do it if the account isn't paid in full. Here's an example of a very explicit message on a statement:

> For the past three months, we have made every reasonable attempt to have you pay this account, to no avail.
>
> As a result, we must advise you that if you do not pay us within 48 hours, in full, we will assign the account to the Collection Bureau of Anderson County, which reports all accounts to three national credit reporting companies.
>
> This means that, EVEN IF YOU DO EVENTUALLY PAY THIS ACCOUNT, THIS WILL SHOW UP ON THEIR RECORDS AS A PAID COLLECTION ITEM, WHICH MEANS THAT ALL OTHER CREDITORS THAT YOU MAY WANT TO DO BUSINESS WITH WILL KNOW THAT YOU ARE A CUSTOMER

WHO HAD TO BE TURNED INTO COLLECTION IN ORDER
TO GET YOU TO PAY.

This can affect whether or not you get any future credit and, if
so, how much.

Wouldn't it be better to pay this account now and avoid all
that unnecessary aggravation and cost?

This is a very direct message. If your debtor doesn't respond to that, you can feel comfortable in knowing that you
made every effort to prevent the final step, which now must
be taken, and if you do lose your customer as a result, it was
unavoidable. Some businesses send their final notice by reg-
istered mail, return receipt requested. This method assures
you that the message is received and helps generate a sense
of urgency within your debtor.

Step 9: Bite the Bullet

If there has been no response to your fourth and final statement by two weeks after you sent it, it's time to do one of
the following:

1. Write off the account from the receivables and cease all
   further collection activity.
2. Use a pre-collection letter service.
3. Use a small claims court.
4. Give the account to a collection attorney.
5. Assign the account to a collection agency.

In Chapter 14, I describe each of these five choices and discuss the advantages and disadvantages of each method.

Regardless of which alternative you select, you must pick
one—no bluffing. Don't say that you're going to assign to
collection in two days and then, when a week goes by, send
out another notice that says this time you're *really* going to
do it. You say what you're going to do and then do it, or don't
bother saying it.

Of all the steps in the billing and collecting system, the toughest parts for most businesses are making the phone calls and biting the bullet at the right time. It's just so easy to procrastinate. But biting the bullet has a ripple effect on your system. If you don't have the discipline to bite the bullet when you should and you hang on to accounts for a few more months, you have no practical incentive to do the earlier steps when or as systematically as you should, so the whole system breaks down.Biting the bullet at four and one-half months, or earlier, forces good collection habits on the business, and that's good.

————————

Conclusion: Biting the bullet on a debtor is like firing an employee: In both cases we wait too long, and at the later stages we don't learn enough that would have changed the same decision made a lot earlier. Systems are nice, and so are guts.

11

Written Communications—What They Can and Can't Do

Written collection messages are the worst form of communication you can select. At their best, they're only one step above no communication at all. They're often a one-way communication that gets trashed and ignored. A phone call or a face-to-face chat are vastly more productive because they're two-way communications. I'm not against written dunning messages. It's just that you have to know what you're up against when attempting to collect with the written word. It's even worse than I've suggested. When sending out a bill, your business—and all businesses—will have three strikes against it.

1. Your bill isn't the only piece of mail your debtor gets. Your bill can easily get lost or thrown away with the junk mail. Much mail does get pitched into the wastebasket after only a cursory, half-second glance.
2. Your mail is competing with mail from direct mail experts, such as *Readers Digest* or Publishers Clearing

House, and your bill doesn't have Ed McMahon on the front promising $2 million if you just open the envelope.

3. Mail from you (your bill) is never good news. It's bad news: Opening the envelope will cost the debtor money.

Because of all these negatives, it makes sense to use billing and collecting techniques that work for the direct mail experts. (You *are* in the direct mail business when you use the mail to try to collect.)

The three direct mail techniques you need in collecting are those that

1. Discourage the mail from being discarded.
2. Encourage the envelope to be opened.
3. Increase the odds of a positive result if the envelope is opened.

Now let's discuss these techniques.

How to Discourage Your Bill From Being Thrown Away or Not Delivered

All your bills probably have your company name and address on the upper left hand corner of the envelope. That's fine for statements 1 and 2. By the third and for all future months, I'd like you to use envelopes that *don't* have that information on them. If your first two bills have been ignored, there's no point in announcing to your debtor, when you send out subsequent bills, "Here's another one you can throw away."

Your first bill should also have imprinted on the upper left-hand corner ADDRESS CORRECTION REQUESTED. If your debtor has moved and notified the post office, you'll get your envelope back with the new address. You can also add FORWARDING POSTAGE GUARANTEED, which means that the envelope will be forwarded directly to the new address. By the third month, I'd leave either message off the envelope because there isn't much point in paying return or forwarding postage each time you send the envelope.

I suggest that you carry two stocks of billing envelopes. Use one type for statements 1 and 2 and have printed on them your return address and your instruction to the post office in case the debtor has moved. The second stock, used for statements 3 and all subsequent bills, shouldn't have your return address imprinted on them. The added outlay for a new stock of envelopes will be paid off easily. Even if you use a computer to do your billing, the computer can be programmed to sort out all statements 1 and 2, at which point envelope 1 is used; all other bills are run and inserted into envelope 2.

How to Encourage the Debtor to Open Your Bill

You don't want to just avoid having the envelope ignored or thrown out; you want to encourage debtors to actively, even eagerly, open the envelope and see what's inside. But you have to avoid using techniques that would constitute a form of harassment. For example, you can't

1. Use a window envelope that has what looks like a check showing through.
2. Write "Past Due" on the envelope.
3. Write "Pay up, you deadbeat."

Six legitimate messages or markings you can write, type, or print on the outside of the envelope that will encourage opening the envelope are:

1. URGENT.
2. PERSONAL. Have you noticed the increase in the

amount of mail marked "Personal," particularly from companies you have never heard of? Companies use this tactic because it works.

3. CONFIDENTIAL.
4. PERSONAL AND CONFIDENTIAL.
5. PLEASE DO NOT FOLD. This one intrigues people; they want to know what's inside that they aren't supposed to fold.
6. Place a yellow check mark on the envelope. The mark makes the envelope stand out.

The size and color of the envelope *may* affect response. Test these techniques by using one group of debtors from a section of the alphabet and compare the results with what you normally get from the rest of the alphabet.

Another billing consideration is *when* during the month you bill, particularly consumer debtors. Many businesses find that it helps to have bills delivered prior to month-end so that the debtor has your bill in the stack when the paycheck comes and bills get paid.

How to Get the Debtor to Pay Once the Envelope Is Opened

Your goals are to get the debtor's attention, avoid being ignored, avoid any misunderstandings, and get paid in full promptly.

1. Make it clear when the bill is to be paid, how much, any discounts or penalties, and, in some cases, the consequences for not paying.
2. Use large print, arrows, reverse printing (white lettering surrounded by black), or a highlighter pen. (I realize that large-volume billing makes some of these ideas useless.)

3. Put a "P.S." at the bottom of the statement. Much of the direct mail you receive has a P.S. at the bottom because the eye travels there more easily than to blocks of copy in the middle of the page.

4. In your business, if there are predictable reasons why debtors think they don't need to pay, to pay you, or to pay in full, *acknowledge* those reasons, like the good salesperson you are, or resistance will persist and you won't be paid.

Let's elaborate on point 4. For example, medical testing labs receive for evaluation tissues and fluids sent to them by doctors and hospitals. The labs seldom see the patients, who typically are unaware of the legal right that the doctor has to order the tests. When the patients get the bill from the lab, their reaction often is, "I didn't order those tests, and even if I did, my insurance would cover it. Go bill the doctor." To dissolve most of that predictable reaction, the *first* bill from the lab must include a statement like the following, in large type, and on a separate piece of paper:

URGENT—PLEASE READ FIRST

Many patients, when they receive our statement, are not aware that our lab performed services for them and that we do not bill the doctor or hospital or wait for insurance.

For these reasons, we feel that it is only fair to let you know that your doctor does have the legal right to request these tests, they were ordered to help assure your health and well-being, and that we do not wait for insurance to take care of this service.

We look to you for the entire amount of this bill, which is due now.

If our service is covered by your insurance, you can use a copy of the enclosed statement to request reimbursement from them.

A return envelope is enclosed for your convenience. Thank you.

This approach, plus billing twice a month, cuts way down on the inevitable misunderstandings that cause a delay in or stop payment. The sheer volume of billing in a large testing lab also mandates the need for the most direct kind of written communications, because phone collecting can't be justified for all these first bills.

Other Useful Ideas About Written Credit and Collection Communications

Signs or Written Notices Don't Get Much Response or Even Notice

Businesses that have customers come to them often have signs, somewhere in the business office, stating the payment policy. These signs help a little, but most customers don't even read them! What's needed is the approach I described earlier in the chapter; namely, give each customer his or her own copy of the policy and get feedback.

Similarly, legions of businesses send out statements with important payment information printed on them, only the information is in small or light type or on the back of the statement. In no case do the words command much attention. These businesses, which invariably find customers ignoring the messages, absolve themselves of blame by announcing, self-righteously, "Well, the warning was there, *if only they would read it.*" That's a big if—big enough to shove an unmanageable accounts receivable through. You can't assume people will read anything. The better assumption is that they won't, so you'd better make extraordinary effort to have important messages read.

Obviously, *how* and *where* the messages are placed are of some importance. Imagine that you're writing ad copy; to get attention at all, you have to write a good headline, and it needs to be big enough to be noticed. You'll improve the odds of your messages being read and acted on if you state not only the message, clearly, but also tell the customers why it's in their interest to read it. In other words, give benefits as well as facts. For example, instead of just stating "Interest is charged on all accounts over 30 days at the rate of 1 percent per month," precede that information with a message such as, "Here's how you can save money now!"

In my consulting work with businesses, one area that almost always is susceptible to clearer communications is the written messages. I suggest that you take a fresh look at *all* your written credit and collection policies, procedures, and messages to customers, in light of the ideas in this chapter. Odds are that you'll easily find a few changes you want to make.

All Written Materials Should Be in the Key Languages of Your Customers

If many of your customers speak a language other than English, as is true in states such as Texas and California, all your written materials should be in all the primary language(s). For example, in San Francisco, which has a polyglot population, messages in Chinese, Japanese, Philippine (Tagalog), and Spanish are useful.

On the other hand, if you're doing collection work on the phone and the debtor claims to not speak English, try saying the word "collection" into the phone in a firm voice. Quite a few such debtors then discover that they can speak a little English.

Motivating Phrases for Collection

Over the years, I've read books that try to demonstrate that certain phrases will produce certain results with debtors and that a number of universal human factors, positive and negative, will be affected by written collection messages. I must share with you my personal bias about these so-called motivating factors: I take them with not just a grain but a mountain of salt. I'll list these factors because they sometimes can help with *debtors who're already below the line* on the Spectrum of Debtors; that is, they're more likely to pay.

I'm skeptical of these motivating phrases and factors

because I don't believe that you can fundamentally motivate anybody to do anything! You can, however, create an environment or a situation in which others choose to motivate themselves. One wag said, "You can lead a horse to water, but you can't make him drink." A wiser observer added, "Yeah, but you can make him awfully thirsty," at which point the horse decides on his own that drinking would be a good idea. In human affairs, managers are better off "motivating" by example and appreciation of efforts. Exhorting the troops to sacrifice for the good of the company doesn't seem to work so well, as the Russians and others are belatedly admitting.

Here are the motivating factors that may be of some use:

1. Save on finance charges
2. Freedom from anxiety
3. Keep a good credit record
4. Retain your honor, honesty, pride
5. Remain a customer
6. Avoid a bad debt record
7. Avoid being turned over to collection

The following sample letters include several of these "motivating" factors:

Sample first letters (or message on statement)

Your balance of $182.50 is now due. A return envelope is enclosed for your convenience.

We appreciate having you as a valued customer.

Thank you.

Sample second letter

Your balance of $182.50 is now past due and needs to be paid in full at this time.

For your convenience, we can accept cash, check, or an approved credit card.

Your prompt attention to this matter will keep your credit record at its present high level.

Thank you.

Sample final letter

Your account is now seriously past due. We have made every effort to invite your payment or communication with us.

Although we would regret losing you as a customer, you must know that our products cannot be delivered unless they are paid for.

THIS ACCOUNT WILL BE TURNED OVER TO MERIT COLLECTION SERVICE IN 72 HOURS IF WE DO NOT HEAR FROM YOU OR RECEIVE PAYMENT IN FULL.

As a result, your credit record may be affected, you may be sued, and additional costs be assessed.

We urge you to avoid all these actions, which we will take, by responding now.

Thank you.

Payment letter—customer is making payments, and you've agreed to the payment schedule. After each payment, to encourage that the payment schedule be maintained, acknowledge the payment and remind the debtor about the next one, so there's no slippage.

Thank you for your regular payment of $100.00.

As you know, your next $100 payment is due May 15, and an envelope is enclosed for your convenience.

Please mark your calendar now as a reminder.

If you can increase the payment amount, we would be happy to give a 5 percent discount for everything over $100. So, if you pay $195 next month, we will credit you with $200.

Please call if you have any questions about this offer.

Thank you.

Final Thoughts

Your advertising department or consultant should look over your written credit and collection messages. These people are experts in selling, and, as I've stated often enough, collecting is selling. Let your advertising copywriters present their ideas on how to sell your debtors into paying and how to create payment policy materials that sell.

After two or at most three written dunning messages, further attempts to collect in writing have very poor odds of success, no matter how brilliantly written they are. But let these two or three messages be as clear and to the point as possible.

Conclusion: The pen is mightier than the sword, but it's weaker than the phone.

12

Phone Techniques—The Geese That Lay the Golden Eggs

In collecting, the phone is ten times more effective than a written communication. That's 1000 percent better! I like odds like that. Your business needs to get on the phone early and skillfully resolve unpaid accounts. The phone is a cost-effective investment that will help retain customers who can be saved. On the other hand, because a phone call is a two-way communication, some responses from debtors are hostile, abusive, or stressful, which leads many collectors to find an excuse to just send another written message instead of using the phone as they know they should.

This chapter is all about the phone as a collection tool. I discuss how to get on the phone, what to say, what responses you'll get, and how to respond to the responses. But before covering any of those topics, I want to discuss how to get *off* the phone. At times you'll find yourself on the phone talking with a debtor who says something you don't know how to respond to. That's an embarrassing situation, and if it happens too often, you'll think hard about getting on the phone again. You have two ways of handling the situation:

1. Thank the debtor for telling you about the problem, and then tell the debtor that you'll discuss it with the boss or the manager and that either they or you will get back to him or her.

2. Say to the debtor, "Excuse me, but I have another call coming in, so let me put you on hold for a moment. I'll get right back to you." While you have the debtor on hold, figure out what to say—since the pressure is off—and pick up the phone and say it. If you can't think of what to say, pick up the phone and use the tactic described in option 1.

Either method gives you a reprieve—a time to think. The debtor doesn't know that there's no other call coming in. (Naturally, you need a hold button on your phone to use this technique.)

Getting on the Phone

Now that you know how to professionally get off the phone, let's prepare how to get on the phone. If you take forever to get around to picking up the phone—you instead always bustle about doing something that looks productive—one way to cut through the resistance is to do what salespeople do:

First call a non-threatening number, such as a recorded weather message, a good client, a friend, your spouse. Call anything to at least get the phone in your hand. Now make a call to your debtor. Your call will be answered by a busy signal, a phone recorder, or a live voice. If it's a recorder, hang up or leave your name, phone number, and the company name. Add, "Please call me about an important matter." Don't say what the matter is because anybody could be listening to the message and such a message would constitute harassment (more on that in Chapter 20).

If a live voice answers, find out who it is; in most states, you can discuss the consumer debt only with the responsible party or the party's spouse. For commercial debts, those owed by a company, you can discuss the nature of the call with anyone who answers.

Be very specific with consumers; if the debtor is Walter Hutton, find out if that's the right Walter Hutton. There could be a Walter A. Hutton, the visiting uncle, Walter Hutton, II, and Walter M. Hutton, the father who owes the bill. After confirming whom you're talking with, give your name and company name. Next, say what you're calling about and ask for the money. All the time be friendly. Here's how the dialogue might go:

"Hi, is this Walter A. Hutton of 89 Melrose Court? Good. Mr. Hutton, my name is Jason Pine from Grocery Employees Credit Union. I'm calling about the $100 payment that is now a month and a half overdue. Would you please write a check for that today and mail it right in?"

In a moment we'll look at the type of response you might get—negative or positive—but for now notice how direct and clear the communication is. The debtor knows exactly what you want and when you want it. This is a good way of asking for money on the phone.

How Not to Ask for Money

Before going on, I want to look at three ways of asking for money on the phone that aren't so good. In fact, they're terrible!

Wrong Way 1

Hello, this is Jason Pine from Grocery Employees Credit Union. How are the kids [or the weather, or the latest ball scores]?

Do not beat around the bush; get to the point. You could be in for a five-minute discussion about each of the five kids. On the other hand, if your debtor is a long-standing customer who you've known personally, there's no harm in making a personal comment before getting down to business.

If you have a collector available who doesn't know the debtor, it's better to turn the call over to that person, so that the contact can be more business oriented.

Wrong Way 2

Hi, this is Jason Pine from Grocery Employees Credit Union. I'm calling about the $100 you owe us from last month. We billed you, but we haven't heard from you. Would you please send us something on the account [or would you please send us a payment]?

Never, never ask for a payment or something on the account because, if you do, *anything* you get is payment or something on the account. Suppose you have the $100 due, you ask for a payment, and in comes $1. You got exactly what you asked for, because anything is something. You'll probably be irritated that the debtor would be so sneaky. But you brought it on yourself. In Chapter 13, I tell you how to handle debtors who tell you they'll send in a payment. For now, I just want to be sure that you don't invite a vague response by the way you ask for payment.

Wrong Way 3

Hello, this is Jason Pine from G.E.C.U., and I'm calling about your overdue $100 payment. I'm sure there's some good reason we haven't heard from you.

Never ask for a reason or what the problem is. Everyone has problems. Do you want to hear my problems? How much time do you have? When you invite a reason or a problem, you increase the odds of hearing one. However, even if you do ask for the payment correctly, you may still get a problem that you have to deal with, but you'll have fewer if you don't invite them.

Debtor Responses

Now that you've discarded any temptation to ask for money badly, let's see what your debtors can say when you do ask them correctly. Typical responses are:

1. Yes, I'll pay.
2. No, I won't pay.
3. A vague response—neither yes nor no.
4. Silence at the end of the phone.
5. "Would you repeat the question?"
6. "No comprendo."

For responses 7 to 100, you've no idea what they'll say. Therefore let's examine the general types of response and how to deal with them.

Negative Response

"No, I'm not going to pay you." This is both good news and bad news. The bad news is that you have a problem. You don't know what the problem is, but you have no doubt that there's no payment coming. This kind of clear communication lets you know where you stand, which brings us to the good news; although you know you have a problem, you also know that you have it now, not later, and the sooner you find out about a problem, the better off you are.

There's no need to spend more time on the account unnecessarily. We haven't found out specifically what the problem is or how to handle it, but this is a general, not a specific, evaluation of phone responses.

Positive Response

"Thank you for reminding me. I'll pay you in full today." This sounds like a collector's dream. You got what you wanted, so go on to the next account.

Nailing Down the Promise

Experienced collectors can tell you that there are plenty of debtors who'll promise you anything you ask, just to get you off the phone. To reduce the likelihood of that happening, use the technique known as Nailing Down the Promise. All it requires is a phone, which is already in your hand, and a calendar.

When you get a promise to pay, say something like this, "That's great, Mr. Debtor. Let's see now, today is the twelfth and the mail service takes about 2 to 3 days, so if you send it today, I'll certainly have your check by the fifteenth. I'll mark my calendar for the fifteenth so I'm sure not to miss it. Thank you very much. Goodbye."

You've now nailed down the promise. If the debtor thought he could get rid of you by an empty promise, he now knows better; you'll be looking for the check. When you use this technique, actually write the debtor's name and the amount promised on your calendar.

If challenged, say that it's not that you don't trust the debtor; it's just that you have so many payments coming in each day that you want to assure the debtor that his payment won't be lost somewhere.

Check Doesn't Arrive

You've now reduced the probability of an empty promise, but you haven't eliminated it. If the check comes in as promised, that's great. But if it doesn't, what do you do? First, let's look at what *not* to do.

1. The check was due the 15th, but you wait another day or two. Wrong. Three days is plenty of time; waiting even one day longer will only prolong the inevitable and show you to be a paper tiger.
2. You send out a letter on the fifteenth reminding the debtor that you didn't get the money. Wrong. A letter costs you several more days, and if a letter or bill had worked, you wouldn't have needed the phone call in the first place.
3. You call up the debtor on the fifteenth and say something like this, "Hello, this is Jason Pine from Grocery Employees Credit Union, calling about the $100 check you said you would send on the twelfth. Well, here it is, the fifteenth, and I can't believe it, the check isn't here. What kind of person would make a promise they wouldn't keep? I wouldn't do that to you. And after all I've done for you to keep your account out of collection. I don't think that's fair on your part. I don't even think you're a good person."

OK, I'll admit I exaggerated a bit in statement 3, but the dialogue makes a point. Please don't indulge in self-righteousness and guilt dumping. It's very easy to get self-righteous about why debtors should pay their bills. After all, you have bills too, and you pay yours or else you don't spend what you don't have. It's only normal to *feel* self-righteous. What's not OK is to *express* it in the collection call. Debtors get self-righteous too about why your prices are so high, all the bills they have to pay, and so on. Two self-righteous people talking to each other are like two ships passing in the night: There's no communication.

The correct response to the debtor who didn't send in the check as promised is this, "Hi, this is Jason Pine from Grocery Employees Credit Union. I'm calling about the $100 you promised on the twelfth. Today is the fifteenth, and we didn't get it." That's it; no guilt, no questions. The ball is now in the debtor's court. Stay silent until the debtor responds.

Again, the debtor has a few options. He could respond, "You didn't get my check because I didn't send it." Whoops. Now you know you have a problem. Bad news, of course, but the good part is that you wasted only three more days finding out about it. Another response could be, "I'm so sorry, I wrote that check, but I left it in my wife's jacket [or some other excuse]." The debtor may be writing the check right now and needs a face-saving excuse. That's fine; give it to him. Tell him you do that all the time also. If you get another promise to pay, that's what you want; and you nail that one down also, for the eighteenth. Thank your debtor and hang up.

One more step. The eighteenth rolls around and the check is still not in your office. What now? Turn the conniving little liar into collection? No. One more phone call; but a phone call with a difference.

You made the last phone call because the debtor said he'd do something but didn't. Remember, I said I'll give almost anyone the benefit of the doubt once. But do you really believe that two broken promises in a row within three days is a coincidence? Not likely. This upcoming phone call will take this reality into account:

"Hi, this is Jason Pine from Grocery Employees Credit Union. You know that check you said you'd send us a second time? Well, we didn't get that one either." Listen for response. If you get a third promise, say, "That's great. If you write the check today and send it in, we'll have it by the twenty-first.

"But I must tell you that if we don't have it by the twenty-first, the account will be turned over to our collection agency on the twenty-second, and we don't like to do that. We much prefer to work with our members ourselves, so won't you please send in the check as you've been promising so we don't have to turn the account over? Thank you."

This is pretty strong stuff. But suppose your debtor still isn't finished trying to work you over and says, "What's the matter, don't you trust me?" The answer is, "Of course, I trust you" [that's a terrible lie, but it doesn't hurt to say it] or "Well, trust really has nothing to do with it. It's just that when our borrowers make two promises in a row that they don't keep, we find that the odds of them keeping the third promise are pretty slim, so our board requires that I turn the account into collection if the check isn't here by the twenty-first. Thank you. Goodbye."

If the twenty-first comes and there's still no check, you do what you said you'd do. If your debtor gets upset, you know that you did everything you reasonably could do; you simply have an above-the-line debtor.

When you collect on the phone, there's no way of knowing in advance what a debtor will say. Some companies have developed "cheat sheets" or scripts that show what to say when a debtor says something. Those scripts may be a good tool for beginning collectors, but I have little faith in them because debtors have an infinite variety of things they can say, assuming what they say is what they're really thinking, and you'd need a very big computer to provide you with the "right response" to any of the millions of debtor responses.

In addition, if you're busy looking for the right, snappy comeback to give your debtors when they give you an excuse, you won't be able to hear what they're saying. You can't listen to the other person when you're ready to give a response to what she said thirty seconds ago.

The Best Technique

Collectors are always looking for better comebacks, but that's looking for magic. (However, several responses or questions are available for using in certain situations. Chapter 18 examines typical debtor excuses.) The best telephone collection technique isn't a technique or comeback at all; it's the willingness to be in communication with the other person and the willingness to *lose*.

Let me explain these strange sounding concepts. When I talk about the willingness to be in communication with the other person, I include what she's saying, what she isn't saying but you detect anyway, and how she's feeling about what she is and isn't saying. When I say I'm willing to lose, that doesn't mean I intend to lose the discussion. It does mean that if the debtor really doesn't intend to pay, I want to make it safe for her to tell me that rather than give me some vague promise or what she thinks I want to hear. The sooner I find out about her real intentions, the better.

The truth is, in a collection dialogue, both sides *make it all up*. Whoever speaks first has no idea what the other person will say and therefore doesn't know what commitments he or she is going to make or how the conversation will end. Therefore, a script is useless. A script also gets in the way of the toughest part of the conversation: listening. How can you possibly respond to the debtor unless you hear *all* of what the debtor isn't as well as is saying?

When I collect, I never have the slightest idea of how I'll respond to the debtor. That point of view, by itself, allows me to *listen*. Although I don't have a script or a prepared comeback, I do have a point of view, which is that you do owe the money and *you* need to do whatever you need to do to take care of it. I'll be flexible where I can, and I'll be guided by our policy on how much leeway to give.

This point of view doesn't come easily. Experienced collectors have as much trouble with it as beginners. But when I demonstrate its concept with role playing, *I always win.* Knowing that you'll always win the battle gives you tremendous power and self-confidence. But we have to define winning. It includes a debtor slamming down the phone and never calling back again. Who wins that one? I do, because I now know I have a debtor with whom further contact would be useless. Out to collection he goes. You see, the end result of your collection calls can never be the bill 100 percent paid in full. It can be your speedy *resolving* of the accounts, which means that those who'll pay will do so quicker, and those who won't will be flushed out faster.

Chapter 16 has more information on role playing. As you'll see there, the *only* way to get your collectors' skill levels to the point that they know they'll always win is through group role playing. That's also the only way they'd be willing to do what I do in front of an audience of fifty or more people, which is announce that I'm going to demonstrate collecting through role playing with a tough debtor and that I'll win every time.

This doesn't mean that I'm any smarter than any other member of the group, because I'm not. It simply means that I've given up the illusion that I can control someone's response. I have no control whatever over the debtor's response. I have control over only my awareness of what they're really saying—but that's enough.

The amateur collector thinks that she can control or motivate the debtor, which is why amateurs lose more often than necessary. I wish I could make this point clearer, but I can't. You'll get the point by doing, not by reading.

Making Time for Calls

Businesses always claim that they don't have enough time to make the collection calls they should. They know the value of the calls, but there are so many other things to do, so many other accounts to handle, etc. Here are solutions to this problem:

1. Hire a part-timer. Part-timers pay for themselves many times over by doing the clerical work while you make the phone calls. If volume permits, hire a full-timer.

2. Make evening and Saturday calls. Consumer calls can be made up to 9:00 P.M.. to reach at home those people who work all day. Don't call at dinnertime; you'll just

annoy people. Calling from 7 to 9:00 P.M. once a week or once a month is a good idea. On Saturdays let people sleep in; call from 10:30 A.M. to noon. For commercial accounts, Saturday is a good day to call because many businesses are open that day.

3. If you have a temporary large backlog of current accounts, retain a collector temporary. Some collection agencies can provide a "gentle collector." Be sure the person you hire is skilled and trained, not just a warm body sent over by some agency.

Reducing Stress

We mentioned that collection phone calls can be stressful. To reduce the stress,

1. Give numerous awards and recognition for good performance.

2. Have physical stress absorbers on hand. A punching bag is great for this purpose. One company I know of bought a six-foot clown, weighted on the bottom, from a toy store. When the clown is hit, it comes right back for more. Another company put a voodoo doll on the wall, with several brightly colored arrows nearby. After a particularly stressful call, the collectors get up and stick an arrow in a delicate spot on the doll, just to get even with the debtor.

3. This sounds unusual, but in many communities you can hire massage specialists who come in and do fifteen minute, fully clothed, neck and shoulder massage for a moderate group rate. It's a great employee benefit or reward.

Conclusion: The correct color for your phones should be gold, as a reflection of their value in collecting money.

13

How to Ask for Money and Not Feel Guilty

I t may appear unnecessary or even condescending to include a separate chapter on how to ask for money. You may wonder what is so difficult; if you want to ask, you just ask. But it is difficult for most people to ask—in plain English and without embarrassment—a customer, client, patient, or borrower to pay, for a number of reasons:

1. Customers might think you don't trust them.
2. Customers might think you're more interested in money than in selling a quality product or service or developing a good relationship.
3. Customers may go to a competitor who has easier payment terms.
4. Even worse, customers may tell all their friends and associates about a competitor who's easier to do business with.
5. Regardless of what might or might not happen, you, the asker, get shortness of breath, sweaty palms, and other physical symptoms any time you have to ask for money.

6. Customers may say something you don't know how to respond to.
7. You may feel sorry for customers with excuses and then hate yourself for buying into their stories.
8. Boss may criticize you for not collecting enough or for customers complaining about your asking them to pay.
9. Customers might get really nasty: scream, curse, threaten to get physical, or even cry.

Regardless of the reason, most people who do ask for money will tell you that it isn't the favorite part of their job.

The discomfort of asking for money usually causes one of the following reactions:

1. You ask in an indirect, evasive manner (examples to follow).
2. You apologize for asking.
3. You become hard-nosed in asking so as to finesse or preempt the potential game player.
4. You avoid asking as much as possible and instead send written dunning messages.

My usual approach in explaining how to do something is to begin by showing how not to do it. This method brings to the listeners' full consciousness the action that has to be eliminated so that they can at least be more aware of, and have greater choice about, whether or not to continue that action.

Common But Ineffective Approaches

When you ask for money, the key point is to be *specific* as to *how much* money you want and *when* you want it. Even if you're specific about these points, you won't always get what you ask for. If you're vague, the results will be worse. Let's discuss the phrases and approaches most commonly used in asking for money but that don't work very well.

"We'd like you to pay all, or at least half." Given that choice, what would you pay?

"You need to pay now, or at the end of the month, for sure." If you give people a choice, few will pick the tougher alternative.

"How much can you pay?" If the debtor doesn't want to pay the full amount, this phrase is the worst possible to use. It's better to ask, "How much are you short the balance?", or "How much time do you need to take care of this in full?" I prefer to have debtors think about payment in full rather than numbers of payments; in other words, the objective, not the method.

"Can you send a payment?" or "Can you send something on the account?" As we stressed in the previous chapter, in wrong way 2 for asking for payment, *never* ask for a payment or something on the account because, if you do, *anything* you get is something or a payment. Let's illustrate this concept again. Suppose your customer owes you $400. You ask for a payment, and in comes $4. You got exactly what you asked for because $4 is definitely "a payment." You also get irritated because your debtor should have known that $4 isn't a reasonable payment on a $400 account. Maybe so, but when you leave the amount completely up to the debtor, who can you blame but yourself for a ridiculous payment?

Because this is such a common error in asking for money, let me take it a step further. Instead of you asking, incorrectly, for a payment, suppose you ask for the money correctly but your debtor promises to send "a payment." How do you respond? Certainly not by thanking the debtor, which only confirms your acceptance of no commitment. What you say, instead, is something like, "That's great. What I need to know is how much you plan to send and when, and we also need to talk about how you plan to take care of the balance." Then, you negotiate. If you don't confront the debtor's vagueness, you're sure to get less money.

"We'll bill you." Don't be such a chicken. Billing is the *last* alternative, not the first. In Chapter 8, I listed strategies for asking for payment at the time the product or service is delivered, beginning with asking for payment in full now, continuing with the offer of an envelope to return the money in, proposing a short payment schedule, and *only* if all else fails, suggesting that you bill the debtor. Unless you provide a billing service, your company isn't in the billing business, and you want to cut down as much as possible on sending bills.

"Don't worry about it." Many bosses of small- or medium-sized companies utter this statement grandiloquently to their customers, typically long-standing customers, to show how appreciative they are of the customers' business and how they fully trust customers to take care of the bill as soon as possible. People who have to collect for bosses like that despise being put in the following situation: They ask a favored customer to pay, so the customer goes straight to the boss, who gives a dispensation with "Don't worry about it." The collector winds up in the middle, embarrassed at least and probably feeling impotent as well.

Bosses in such companies often give their business office people a mixed message: "Don't hassle our good customers" yet "Why aren't you collecting more money for me?"

This solution isn't good for the boss, who isn't getting paid as he should, for the collectors, who are being second-guessed and disempowered in their collection work, and even customers, who receive signals that this company has wishy-washy payment policies or, even better for them, easy pickings on payment. Nobody wins.

To correct this no-win situation, the company must initiate several responses. First:

The boss should determine the collection policy and agree to leave its implementation entirely in the hands of the business office. If the customer does get to the boss, to complain about how tough the collector is, the boss should tell the customer that it's out of her hands—she's so nice that her CPA insists that only the business office can implement payment policy—please see them about the problem.

The boss should also assure the customer that the business office is very understanding and is quite experienced in working with customers who have a temporary financial problem. The boss should add that other customers, in a similar situation, after talking with the business manager, were so pleased with the outcome that they returned to the boss to tell her how helpful the business manager was. This reassurance, combined with shunting the customer off to someone else (the business manager), gets the boss off the hook and allows the bill to be dealt with in a professional manner.

Third, if the boss is unwilling to take the steps just described, the business manager should record all accounts that the boss told customers not to worry about. When the boss asks why collections aren't so good, the manager can present these accounts to the boss, saying, "These are *your* accounts." Business managers who've use this tactic report that it usually opens up the boss's mind and usually deters him from interfering again with the collection process.

Fourth, businesses make extreme efforts to set out credit and collection policies and communicate them in written and verbal forms so that customers will understand and comply with them. But one communication that never seems to be misunderstood is "Don't worry about it." Once those words are uttered, not a customer around will misunderstand them. Even if the payment policy was crystal clear, if anyone says this "don't" phrase, the customers' reaction will be, "Don't worry about it? You got it. I won't. Thanks a lot. I really enjoy doing business with you."

Finally, if the customer won't agree to a reasonable payment plan and asks to see the boss, the collector shouldn't refuse this request outright because doing it will surely infuriate the customer. Instead, the collector should say, "My boss is delighted to talk with customers, particularly a good friend like you, about anything, including our credit and collection policy. But when it comes to specifics on how a bill is to be taken care of, I assure you he'll send you to me to work it out, so why don't we try to do that now?" The customer may still insist on seeing the boss, but the collector will be secure, we hope, in the certainty of the boss listening politely to the customer, answering with something like the first response we discussed, and sending the customer back to the collector.

"Would you...ah, uh...do you think you, you know, could...uh... well, sort of, pay something today, if that's not, you know, too much...well, like, trouble?"

Pretty bad, isn't it? There's no need to apologize or be vague.

"There must be some good reason why you haven't paid this yet." I discussed this response in the previous chapter on phone technique. I'm repeating it because there is such a strong tendency to acknowledge the wrong thing. In Chapter 15, Communication Secrets of the Real Pros, I'll examine the power of acknowledgment as a major tool of communication. But you don't want to acknowledge a reality, such as nonpayment, to give it legitimacy or primacy over the need to pay. Don't focus on the excuses, which can be endless and manufactured. Deal with the options for solving the problem.

"People need to pay their bills. We have expenses, too, you know." No self-righteousness, please. Any form of guilt dumping is counterproductive.

"The cost today is $1000. I'm sure you don't carry around that kind of money." The two big messages in this response are don't ask in a negative way, and, particularly with a "big" bill, don't follow the strong tendency to assume that some debtors won't have the money. The truth is that *you have no idea who can and who can't pay.* You may think you know, but you don't.

With consumer debtors, you may make a judgment based on how they're dressed, where they live, or what job they have. Experience proves that many poorly dressed people take pride in paying bills promptly, whereas quite a few wealthy people are niggardly about paying for their purchases.

With commercial accounts, those owed by companies, rather than individual consumers, you should be in a better position to determine, by checking their payment habits with other creditors, their likelihood of paying you. But even established business accounts can go sour. The business may fall on hard times, have an embezzlement or a fire, or face any number of problems that may make its previously spotless payment record very spotted. Don't assume anything. Regardless of the amount of a big bill, *always* begin by asking for it all. The good negotiator doesn't begin by giving away bargaining points in advance.

One day when I was a kid growing up in Lancaster, Pennsylvania, in the heart of the Amish country, I was standing outside the Cadillac dealership when a fellow who looked like a farmer walked in, brushed the dirt off his overalls, asked to see the floor models, and peeled off cash from a wad of bills to pay in full for his new Caddy. I was shocked that someone so "poor" could do that, but the incident began the process of teaching me to not judge the book only by the cover.

Correct Techniques

As you can see, there's a wondrous variety of ways to ask badly for money. I hope this examination of the main ones will encourage you to drop them entirely from your repertoire. To replace them, use the following specific words and phrases to ask for money correctly, in a clear-cut sequence of steps.

First, have a philosophy, one that sounds obvious or even banal: You have the right to ask for money. I bring up this point because I've talked many people whose job includes asking for payment who felt that they didn't have full permission to ask for money. They preferred that the customer bring it up first.When I speak of the "right" to ask for money, I position it between the negativeness of not asking, for whatever reason, and the self-righteousness of demanding payment.

The so-called right derives from the fact that in this country, if you buy a product or service, you have to pay for it. This relationship is so strong that if someone buys something and doesn't pay, and you go to a court of law to enforce payment of the debt, you'll almost always win, even though there may be nothing in writing about payment. Your lawyer can define exactly what that implied obligation is all about. It always helps to have understandings about money in writing, but, as you can see, you're on unshakable grounds when you ask for payment on a debt.

There are five main phrases to use when asking a debtor to pay.

1. *Pay.* Asking someone to pay is perfectly OK, but the word is so blunt that many collectors shy away from it. Fortunately, over the years, several other ways of saying "pay" that have the same meaning but sound a little less direct have been developed.
2. *Clear.* Say, "We'd appreciate it if you would clear your account."
3. *Handle.* "You can handle this by cash or check, whichever you prefer."
4. *Take care of.* Same phraseology as above.
5. *Keep your account current.* Some offices get a bit sophisticated and say to their overdue accounts, "We'd appreciate it if you would bring your account current." If your debtor doesn't know what that means, you can explain that it means "pay."

After you ask your debtor to pay, clear, handle, take care of, or bring the account current, the next words relate to how they can do so. Say, "Would you rather take care of that today by cash, check, or credit card [or whatever other methods of payment you allow, including barter]?"

The next step is to *shut up*. This is the notorious psychological pause. You can look at the debtor, if you're face-to-face, or hand him a pen, but don't say a word. The ball, obviously, is in his court, and he has to commit to something, if only an excuse for not paying. If you talk at this point, you defer the need to confront that decision and you delay resolving the account one way or the other. Then, depending on what the debtor says, you accept it, reject it, or negotiate. So, to ask for money:

1. State the amount of the bill.
2. Ask for it all now.
3. Give choices of methods of payment in full now.
4. Wait for a response.

As you know, the responses can be both highly creative and deceptive. We'll deal with them in Chapter 16, where you'll learn to role play your way to handling any debtor excuse, and Chapter 17, where we'll look at classic games and the more effective, scripted responses. The scripts aren't word for word, but they do get you started in forcing the debtor to face reality.

I don't want to leave the subject of how to ask for money without telling you about the worst situation I ever encountered in asking for money. I'll then show you how best to handle it.

I did a one-day consulting assignment at Memorial-Sloan Kettering Hospital in Manhattan—the nation's largest cancer hospital and research center. Much of the day was spent talking about how to appropriately ask for money in a situation that's as difficult as any I know: The debtor is a cancer victim who's probably in much pain, who has incredibly large bills, and who's likely to die. If that isn't an uncomfortable enough situation, I don't know what is. Still, the money has to be dealt with; doing so involves a two-step approach.

Because the situation is awkward and you'll probably feel uncomfortable, begin by acknowledging both the situation and your feelings, like this: "Discussing money under these circumstances is, frankly, something I wish we didn't have to do." Then offer the following choice: "So, if you'd rather discuss this at another time or if you prefer that I talk with another member of the family, I'd be happy to do that."

You've given the debtor the choice as to when to discuss the bill and with whom, but you've brought up the subject in a way that preserves the patient's options and dignity as well as your humanity.

A number of examples in this book are from the world of doctors and hospitals because I've found that these people live in a world of economic fantasy, to a degree found in few other business sectors. Chapter 22 looks at more of their problems and solutions.

---

*Conclusion: Asking for money is **not** like undergoing a root canal without anesthesia; it only seems that way.*

14

The End of the Road—What to Do When You Can't Collect

In handling unpaid accounts, there comes a time when you have to quit working on an account. That time can come early in the collection process, as with a debtor who goes bankrupt one week after doing business or a debtor who turns out to be a complete skip. Other accounts will string you along for a few months, either with just enough payment to forestall firm collection action or a series of believable stories that have the same effect.

Recall that in Chapter 10 I suggested that an average of four and one-half months of billing and collection calls is enough. If you don't know where you stand by that time, waiting longer won't improve most accounts. You have five ways of disposing of your unpaid accounts: (1) write them off and forget them, (2) use a pre-collection letter service, (3) use a small-claims court action, (4) give the accounts to an attorney, or (5) assign the accounts to a collection agency.

Let's now discuss each option, including the advantages as

well as the disadvantages. I'll also evaluate the options as to cost and the likelihood of success.

Write Off Account and Forget It

This option is used best when you have a small unpaid balance, such as $5, that costs you more to collect than it's worth. Businesses also use a write-off on a touchy account, one that's politically or economically powerful. The perceived fallout of pressing for payment is seen as too risky to be worth the money received. In my view, businesses are often too eager to write off such sensitive accounts. Such action carries with it the probability of perpetuating the conduct that caused the write-off in the first place.

Certain groups of businesses, such as CPAs and lawyers, are known to write off massive groups of accounts, out of a general notion that any stronger action would be bad for business. This attitude has been changing in recent years; more of these formerly benign businesses are demanding payment, or else.

The advantage of a write-off is that you spend no more time on the account; you can devote time to accounts more likely to pay. The disadvantage is similarly straightforward: you won't get paid.

Precollection Letter Service

A letter service consists of one or more letters from a third party (someone other than the credit grantor), directing the debtor to pay the money owed, directly to the creditor. Some services may include a phone call, either by a machine or a real person. Another variation is a letter from an attorney at the end of the previous dunning letters.

Letter services are available from companies that sell only this service, or they can be purchased from collection agencies that offer them, usually for the purpose of getting the accounts that don't respond to the letters and getting them sooner. If a collection agency provides the letter service, you may have the choice of having accounts that don't pay after the letter demands going automatically into the collection agency for collection on a contingency fee basis (you pay nothing unless they collect) or having the right to assign to the service only those accounts you want placed for collection.

One to five letters, seldom more, can be sent. A collection agency may charge you nothing for sending one letter, in the hopes of getting your accounts assigned for "regular" collection; a letter service may charge $5 to $15 per account. A letter service offers three advantages: (1) involvement of a third party, (2) low cost, and (3) other options.

The very powerful third-party involvement advantage applies to all the options except write-off. When you bring in a third party, you're sending a clear message that the matter is out of your hands, you're willing to bring in a specialist, you're willing to risk loss of the customer—in other words, you mean business.

Whatever the perceived message, the fact is that an account handled by any third party will pay quicker than if the creditor does the work. Even more to the point, if you call an account as a third party, you will be more successful in collecting than if you called the same account at the same time in the collection cycle but represented yourself as the creditor instead of the third party.

Other than writing the account off, a letter service is the least expensive option. Also, a letter service offers several options. You may have a choice of the messages used in the letters. The money goes directly to you; it doesn't get held in a trust account for a few weeks, as happens with some agencies and legal options. Finally, because of the low cost, there's an incentive to bite the bullet sooner than with any other option.

The letter service, however, also has several disadvantages. First, letter services don't work on skips. If you have a bad address, no letter will be delivered. Also, the turnover in letter service salespeople is notorious. Ask for references and find out about how your account will be serviced.

A third disadvantages is that the letter service company may try to oversell you on the grounds that the more you buy, the lower the cost per account. They often have a meaningless double-your-money guarantee to back up their claims. I say meaningless because at a cost per account of, say, $10 each, it takes very little in account recovery to give you double your cost. Those accounts might have had a much higher net recovery if another option were chosen. Don't decide just on low cost.If you use a letter service as one of your options, I suggest you buy no more than what you can reasonably use in six months; after that period, evaluate the results.

If you wait the typical six to ten months or more to place accounts, a letter service will probably be a complete waste of money and, worse, time. A consumer or business that has stalled you that long needs the intervention of a more direct option than a series of letters. A letter service is an effective weapon in your collection arsenal, if you use the following three-step approach:

1. Hire a service that sends two letters, three maximum, because if your debtor ignores the first two letters, experience shows clearly that the odds of getting results on the third letter are slim, so you're wasting precious time. Four letters are not twice as much for your money as two letters.

2. Keep the interval between letters short. Thirty days is too long; ten days is much better. At most, use a two-week or semimonthly interval.

3. Turn over accounts ten days after the second month of billing or, at most, ten days after the third month.

The letter service "creams" the easier-to-collect accounts, at the lowest possible cost. Those accounts that don't respond can go to one of the remaining options for biting the bullet. This scenario doesn't mean that all unpaid accounts should go first to a letter service. You shouldn't include skips, some sensitive accounts, accounts that are making acceptable payments, larger accounts that should be handled internally by phone, etc.

Most of the remaining accounts can go quickly into a collection letter service, particularly if you have many of them. I prefer that you use a letter service provided by a collection agency so that you can quickly, even automatically, place those accounts that don't respond to letters immediately into the hands of a professional telephone collector, thereby maintaining the momentum and the urgency that the letters promised.

Because letter services cost so little, creditors tend to use them earlier in the collection cycle than any other option, which naturally results in a higher recovery than other options. This combination of low cost and high recovery (but only when used *early*) makes letter services an important tool. Many businesses have never heard of letter service, have never used them, or have used them badly, with negative results. I hope this analysis provides a new perspective.

A Small-Claims Court (SCC)

A small-claims court is aptly named The People's Court because anyone can file suit there, without representation by attorney. If you file an SCC action, Judge Wapner won't preside, but your experience will be fairly similar to that on an episode of his show. Very few businesses that could and should use the court actually do, usually because they're unfamiliar with the process.

Books on this subject are available, but I'm going to tell you what you need to get started in using your small-claims court (I won't present every detail or variation in the fifty states).

For precise information about the procedure in your county, go to the SCC office of the county court house and obtain whatever information they have. Some SCC clerks aren't helpful at all; but that's not their fault. If the clerk is evasive about the process, it's probably because local attorneys, who don't appreciate the competition SCC actions present, have been leaning on the clerk to be less than helpful.

Before describing the basic process, I want to list the considerable advantages of SCC, and the few disadvantages.

Advantages

1. Low cost. In most courts, $50 or less covers the entire cost of filing a claim and having papers served on the defendant.

2. Prompt response by debtors. Nationwide, 30 percent of the defendants sued pay up as soon as they're notified through a process server of an impending court action. This response isn't surprising. When debtors see that you're serious enough about getting paid to sue, many realize for the first time, that they're going to have to pay, so they might as well get it over with. In other words, any denial mechanism they were using to stall you up to that point is destroyed by that one blinding blast of reality called a lawsuit.

3. Judgment by default. An additional 20 percent of the defendants won't even bother to show up in court, so you get a judgment by default; you win automatically. However, getting a judgment isn't the same as getting money, as you'll see when I discuss disadvantages, but it's a major step forward.

4. High dollar amount allowed. The dollar amount you can sue for, although varying by county and state, is usually several thousand dollars. For many businesses, most of their unpaid accounts fall below the SCC's

upper limit. (For larger amounts, sue in the municipal or superior court.)

5. No need for a lawyer to represent you.
6. Straightforward language and procedure, designed for laypeople, not lawyers.
7. Little time involved. The whole process doesn't take much time. Most disputes are heard in court within a month or two from the time the complaint is filed, and the judge usually renders a decision within a few days of the courtroom presentation.
8. Boss normally doesn't have to appear, just the "keeper of the records," who's usually the business manager.

Disadvantages

1. Judgment. A judgment that can't be converted into money is worthless; so don't bother suing a debtor with no apparent assets. (However, in some instances the judgment is worthwhile, as we discuss shortly.)
2. Skip. If your consumer debtor has skipped, you can't serve the suit papers.
3. Small account balance. Some other bite the bullet option may be more practical if the account balance is small, even though you can usually get the debtor to pay court cost and filing fees if you win the case.

If you go to court and win, the judgment can be a powerful tool for getting your money. However, in some states the judgment is almost meaningless; Texas, for example, is known as a debtor's haven. But in those states that enforce judgments, your judgment can be used to:

1. Garnish wages.
2. Place a lien on physical assets, such as the debtor's house, which means that he then can't sell or refinance the assets before paying you.

3. Obtain a "keeper" or a "till tap" on a business debtor with a cash register, such as a restaurant. A sheriff goes out to the business with the judgment and keeps cleaning out the register until the bill is paid off.

4. Apply a bank levy, which allows you to clean out the debtor's bank account to satisfy the amount shown in your judgment. The first time you get a check from a debtor, make a copy of it or record the bank, branch, and account number because that's what you need to find and secure the money in the debtor's account if you win a judgment. If your debtor doesn't volunteer information about sources of payment, the process of discovery called an Order of Examination requires the debtor to come to court and truthfully answer your questions about income, property, and assets. If the debtor lies, she is subject to the penalty for perjury. If she fails to appear, she is subject to contempt of court penalties, including arrest and jail, with bail set at what is owed you. If you win a judgment and can't collect on it, the *last* resort is to assign the judgment to a collection agency. You'll get only 50 percent of what they collect, but it won't cost you anything if they fail to collect.

I strongly encourage all businesses to become familiar with the SCC option if they've never tried it. It's much easier than learning to program your VCR, and it's surprisingly rewarding.Some businesses avoid any kind of legal action because they fear some kind of backlash regarding their public image or loss of liability insurance in case of a countersuit. But when a few of these brave souls do sue, they're relieved to find that it usually *helps* their image. Chronic debtors get the message that they can't, with impunity, ignore your reasonable demands for payment. Your willingness to sue can help create a businesslike attitude about payment of bills that helps prevent collection problems from occurring the first place. Honest debtors have nothing to fear from a business that sues only as a last resort. Credit criminals will be more impressed, but you don't want their business anyway.

Attorney

You can hire an attorney to file suit on an account for you in a court other than a small-claims court. But a far less expensive use of an attorney is to hire one to send dunning letters to your debtors on the attorney's stationery. The advantage of the letter is that it's not only relatively inexpensive, but, more importantly, a letter from an attorney, unlike regular bills from you, tends to get opened. Have you ever received a letter from an attorney you didn't know? I'll bet you opened it, because in this litigious society, you know that to ignore a legal-looking notice could result in a fine, repossession of physical assets, or worse.

The disadvantage of using an attorney for collection work is that often an attorney has her or his own collection problems. Also, most lawyers have no skiptracing skills. But if you're selective, and particularly if you pick an attorney who specializes in collection work, you should get your money's worth.

One more point: this country, which many consider lawyer-heavy already, continues to churn out more lawyers every year, and many of them don't get jobs at the high-paying law firms. Many of these freshly minted attorneys are scrambling for business—any business. I suggest that you look up a few such attorneys (your local Bar Association can identify them) and offer some of your collection work in return for a good rate.

Collection Agency

Professional bill collectors are everywhere. Their activities are regulated by the Federal Fair Debt Collection Practices

Act; 3500 of them are members of the American Collectors Association. Agencies work on a contingent fee, which means that they don't charge anything unless they collect. Then the fee is usually from 30 to 50 percent on consumer accounts or as low as 15 percent on large commercial accounts (owed by a business to another business).

If an agency can't collect for you by use of the mails or persuasion by phone, and if there are sufficient assets and a large enough account, it may recommend suing. Agency personnel will do the work, and you'll probably be asked to advance the court costs and attorney fees. The suit will be brought in a court higher than a small-claims court.

Of all the bite the bullet alternatives, a collection agency offers the best odds of returning the most net dollars back to you, after its fee is deducted. (Not surprising because agencies do specialize in collections.)

I'm not suggesting that all accounts should go to an agency, certainly not the smaller accounts. However, countless businesses with accounts they considered absolutely uncollectable turned them over to a collection agency and were then paid shortly afterward.

Advantages

Hiring a collection party offers you three primary advantages. An agency is a particularly powerful third party. With an agency, the debtor does not usually know all the resources that can be brought to bear or the consequences of not cooperating. This fear of the unknown is a mighty motivator. Another advantage is that if you don't like making phone calls or don't have enough time to make them, collection agency people spend all day on the phone. They've heard all the excuses, and their experience has made them skilled in dealing with objections.

Finally, a collection agency is the best option for your skip accounts. The agency uses all available tools for you, including the public library, the assessor's office, and other resources away from the office. The agency people's experience enables them to be good at following a trail, if there is one, for either a lost debtor or for finding assets the debtor prefers you didn't know about. If your debtor leaves the area and you know where he or she has gone, an agency can "forward" the account to an agency in the debtor's new location, at no added cost to you.

Disadvantages

The main disadvantage of a collection agency is that it takes a big bite out of every dollar it collects, which irritates many businesses that use them. Agencies justify that fee by explaining that all the businesses' accounts are worked on at the agency's expense, so that for accounts that turn out uncollectible, the creditor hasn't paid a dime.

What often happens when you use an agency is that a debtor, finally realizing that you're serious about getting paid, calls you in panic, promises to pay, and asks you to call off the dogs. Don't go for it; if you do, the debtor will simply play you off against the agency, which buys her more time. Tell your debtor that her refusal to cooperate with you forced you to call in specialists, and now you'll have to deal with them. It's out of your hands. If your debtor is a former friend whom you feel guilty about turning into collection, tell her that the agency requires you to stay out of it; that lets you off the hook, although the statement isn't true.

Some businesses' accounting systems are so messed up that they don't know which accounts are paid and which aren't, so they turn them all into collection. The agency will charge you about half the normal fee for these accounts they demonstrate were paid prior to your assigning to the agency, so turn over only those accounts you know aren't paid.

Businesses often ask how to pick a good agency. That question isn't so easy to answer, and the traditional wisdom gets you only so far. I'd insist on talking to some clients who've used the agency for some time. I'd want the agency to be using one of the computerized systems that do accounting, record control, and many other automated features that free up the collectors to use the phone. Ideally the agency will be a member of the American Collectors Association.

If you have many accounts, use two agencies; the competition encourages them to work a bit harder to get more of your business. Don't use more than two agencies because that adds no more competitive benefit and increases your accounting problems. If one agency shows consistently poor results, respond first by giving more to the better agency. If that doesn't help, replace the weaker one completely with a new agency.

Do not select an agency based on which one gives you the lowest contingent fee. That is the worst possible criterion. You get what you pay for. What matters is not rate but the net dollars returned to you after the fee has been deducted. In other words, the recovery percentage rate is far more important to you than the fee. For example, based on ten $100 accounts totalling $1000, agency A collects 25 percent, or $250, at a 25 percent fee, returning $187.50 to you. Agency B collects 40 percent, or $400, at a 40 percent fee, returning $240 to you. Paying the higher fee doesn't guarantee better recoveries, but the odds favor it.

All five options for biting the bullet have now been examined. I suggest you try them all, and try them in combination. I've said that the average business waits twice as long as it should before making the decision to bite the bullet. Here's a chart that may help you justify making the decision to bite the bullet sooner.

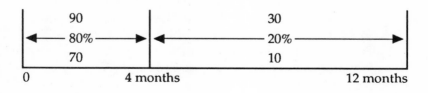

This chart shows the collectibility of accounts over time. Everyone knows that unpaid accounts aren't like fine wines or cheese; they don't improve with age. They rapidly become *less* collectible as the calendar pages turn. The chart shows that accounts four to twelve months old are about 20 percent collectible. This percentage varies by company, industry, and every other variable you care to mention, so there's no point in quibbling about the exact percentage, as we'll see shortly. For you, the collectibility of accounts four to twelve months old may be 30 or 10 percent.

Now let's look at accounts averaging up to four months old; they're approximately 80 percent collectible. For you, they may be 90 or 70 percent, but again, the exact percentage doesn't matter. What does matter is the *relationship* between these two classes of accounts. Obviously, the older accounts are less collectible than the newer accounts, and because you don't have enough time to work on them all with equal vigor, you have to concentrate on the earlier ones and give up on the older ones.

I know this hurts—if you continue to work on the older accounts, you'd collect some of them, about 20 percent. But that *same investment of time and money* in the newer accounts produces an 80 percent return, which is why you have to bite the bullet sooner. This is the logical, analytical, left-brain, irrefutable reason why you must do what is in your interest. Of course your right brain objects strenuously. It just hates to give up. It prefers that collection be an emotional experience, not a business decision.

But not only are the older accounts tougher to collect, they produce far more stress on your collector, so again, there's only bad things to say for whacking away at old, moldy accounts. Give them up. Remember that you win more by being willing to lose a few. The chart demonstrates the wisdom of the card player who knows when to hold 'em and when to fold 'em. In managing your accounts, you aren't gambling, but you're certainly, unavoidably involved in playing the odds. Hanging on to your accounts nine to ten months instead of three to four is like playing lotto; you might possibly win a huge jackpot, but the odds are you'll lose consistently. The amateur looks at the payoff; the professional considers *only* the odds.

There's also an accounting consideration involved in biting the bullet. Many businesses, when turning an account over to some third party, wonder about whether they should write the account off their accounts receivable or wait to see if it will be collected. Accountants usually recommend that an account turned over for collection be written off the accounts receivable entirely. Then, if any money does come in, it should be posted on the profit and loss records as an income item. If you leave the account on the balance sheet as an asset, you'll be overstating your real assets.

Some businesses also ask whether there might be some tax benefit in turning an account into collection. The answer is no. Your action already has tax implications. When you remove an account from your receivables to a third-party collector, you're simply confirming the loss of income that you'd otherwise have paid taxes on. I'd rather have the revenue and pay the taxes than be beaten out of that income. A $25 tax on $100 in income leaves $75; a $100 writeoff leaves nothing. The $100 collected goes right to income because the cost of producing the product or service has already been expended.

Biting the bullet is the single toughest part of your billing and collecting system to implement in a systematic, professional way. To make it easier, you should have criteria for making exceptions. Those criteria must be tough or you'll have too many exceptions and not enough system.

Conclusion: A poem (sort of):
If you want to collect all your unpaid accounts,
Whether or not they're a ton or an ounce,
Consider the fate of a ball dropped on slate,
There's less and less life after each hopeful bounce.

15

Communication Secrets of the Real Pros

What distinguishes professional, skilled collectors from the scared, uncomfortable amateurs is what separates beginning salespeople from the self-assured pros. Part of the difference is sheer experience, but the other part is an understanding of psychology and how to systematically use it when dealing with people. Techniques are wonderful, and you need all you can get, but your techniques will get you only so far unless you know how to deal with resistance to your techniques.

The adversary—whether a debtor or a sales prospect—has a formidable repertoire of defenses against paying or buying. Or the adversary may be persuaded to pay or buy, but not necessarily from you. This chapter describes the five chief psychological tools you'll need to become a better collector.

Acknowledgment

"Acknowledgment" is a fancy word for an activity we all do. It can be defined as a form of feedback to another person of what you observe him or her saying, doing, or feeling. Acknowledgment comes in both positive and negative forms, with powerful effects that are either postive or negative.

A real-world positive acknowledgment is saying "Good morning" to your associates at the beginning of the day. This greeting implies that you recognize and welcome the other person. It usually produces a positive feeling, and the receiver normally reciprocates with her or his own words of recognition. Animals do this acknowledgment all the time, often with elaborate nose touching, tail wagging, or sniffing rituals that may go on for a long time.

A negative acknowledgment occurs, for example, when a person who usually says "Good morning" goes right by you and doesn't say a word. You'll probably notice that immediately and wonder what is wrong, either with the other person or with you. As another example, suppose you're at a restaurant and you're hungry, but the restaurant is short-staffed so you're ignored for five minutes. However, this event can be a positive acknowledgment if the waiters and waitresses, even if they're swamped, take five seconds while passing by you to say, "I'll be with you in just a moment."

Acknowledgment, whether positive or negative, affects how we feel about others. In collecting, much of the communications among people are negative. The positive acknowledgment neutralizes the feeling associated with the statement. Suppose you ask a debtor to pay and he becomes upset. The problem then immediately becomes one of dealing with an upset person. Logic is of very little use. Saying "You shouldn't be upset" to someone who obviously is only makes matters worse.Instead, acknowledge the upset. Say something like, "I'm very sorry that I upset you. I really didn't mean to do that." Continue in this way until your debtor appreciates that you're fully aware of the upset. Until you acknowledge that upset feeling, the debtor is literally unable to focus rationally on logic and the reality of the debt. The feeling overwhelms the mind.

As we discussed earlier, psychologists divide the mind into

two parts: left brain and right brain. The left brain is our logical, analytical, rational part. The left brain is very good at arithmetic and other kinds of logical thinking. The right brain is the emotional or intuitive part; the part that "wants to sleep on a decision." We all have both sides of the brain, but some of us (about 45 percent) are more predominately right brain, others (another 45 percent) are more left brain, and the remaining 10 percent are equal. When we notice someone becoming highly emotional (right-brained), we consider them "out of their minds" (left-brained).

In the worlds of selling and collecting, where there's a high degree of resistance, the debtor's left brain will never hear the logic of your argument unless you first neutralize the feeling associated with his objection to paying. Specifically, when a debtor disagrees with you, you always agree with him. What you're agreeing with is his feelings, not the refusal to pay.

We look at examples of how to use acknowledgment later, when I show you how to handle objections, but the following example illustrates this important point.

> Debtor: I don't see why I should pay your interest charge.

> Collector: That's a perfectly reasonable objection and you're not the first customer to bring it up. I'm going to do my very best to explain this in a way that makes sense to you. OK?

Now give an explanation. Can you see that this approach, which brings the two of you closer together in your communication, always beats the approach whereby you argue with a debtor who's defensive or argumentative?

Hurting Someone's Feelings

This approach is very tricky. Often a collector will say (or think), "I want to ask the debtors to pay, but I don't want to upset them or hurt their feelings in the process because if I do, instead of getting my money, I'll only cause a delay in payment and get upset customers." This kind of thinking, which is *very* common, leads to paralysis.

Simply put, the problem is how do you ask someone to pay without hurting her feelings? The answer is you can't. You have no certainty about your impact on another person. In fact, if you're talking to a group of twenty people, each person will react differently, even though each one heard and saw the same person, you. To be more blunt about this, you can't force your niceness on someone else. Here's a good example. Consider a time when you called up a debtor and asked them, as nicely and sweetly as possible, to pay. Your voice may have been bubbly and upbeat, or highly apologetic for asking, yet the debtor cursed you! You then asked yourself, "What in the world did I say that produced such a strong reaction?" The answer is that it was nothing you said; it was what the debtor added to your gentle communication that produced the upset, loss of control, and your getting sworn at.

So there's no way of controlling another person's reaction to what you say. Therefore, say what you need to say, in plain English, with no beating around the bush, and you'll get the best result. You can't hurt someone else's feelings, but that doesn't give you license to be as obnoxious as you know how. When you hear yourself saying, "What's a nice way of saying this strong message to this debtor," the answer is to say it. If you're evasive or circumspect, you get indecisive results.

Some experienced collectors say that when you collect, you should set your feelings aside. I disagree. As human beings we have feelings. How can you have them and set them aside at the same time? Doing so makes a great formula for stress. Some collectors also feel that you "shouldn't take it personally." This is really a variation of the previous point. Since you're a person, how can you not take it personally? Of course, you don't deal with debtors by coming unglued yourself—you channel your feelings in productive ways, as you'll see shortly.

Hierarchy of Communication

This technique is simple and straightforward. In communicating, you have four options:

1. No communication (cheapest)
2. Writing
3. Phoning
4. Face-to-face contact (most expensive)

Face-to-face contact is the best way of communicating because you can hear the person and she can hear you, and you can also see the debtor's expressions, actions, and body language. The phone is less expensive than visiting each debtor in person. Although you don't receive any visual signals, you and the debtor can hear each other's words and inflections. Again, in collecting, the phone is about ten times more effective than writing.

Written communications are better than none at all, but because they form a one-way street they don't deal with the resistance that may arise. Still, for large-volume, low-cost communications, writing is the way to go.

Bridging

Here we discuss the most useful techniques: how to handle objections. Professional collectors not only don't fear debtors who give them a bad time, they almost welcome the resistance. Why? As we saw in Chapter 9, resistance quickly defines where a debtor is in the Spectrum of Debtors, and in turn we can then more quickly resolve the account. Also, the professional collector, when faced with resistance, loves the challenge, the game, the chase, almost the fun of it.

When confronted by an objection to paying, most collectors use a two-step approach. First, restate the objection so the debtor knows you understand him. Then give the debtor a terrific answer that leaves him transformed and eager to pay. This is a nice theory, but it doesn't work too well. Actually, the best way to handle objections, stalls, excuses, or any kind of resistance is to use a *three*-step procedure.

Face the Objection

First you'll encounter the objection. Typical ones are "I don't like your policy around here." "Times must be tough for you. I'll go where they aren't so worried about money." "Your competitor doesn't do this." "You're no better than a finance company." "Can I start with this payment policy next time?" "I'll report you to the Better Business Bureau."

Bridge From Objection to Answer

This is the key step—the one most people leave out. The bridge acknowledges the *feeling* associated with the question or objection so that the debtor can hear what the answer is when the collector finally delivers it in step 3. Excellent bridges include, "That's an excellent question." "I know pretty much how you feel." "I don't blame you for saying that." "I wish we could do it that way." "Obviously you have a good reason why you feel that way." "Many people have said that." "It certainly seems that way." "Yes, that's true."

Sometimes you don't bridge at all, just give a direct response. The best time to use this tactic is when a debtor challenges your price or fee with, "How come your price on that is so high?" Just say, "We're very proud of our prices." This usually ends the discussion, and your comment is neither defensive nor argumentative. Ultimately there can be no "justification" for any price or charge, but there are certainly people who feel those charges are "too high."

Give the Answers

Once you've made a bridging statement, you can then give an answer that tends to put the objection to rest. For example,

"Our business manager (or CPA) requires that we do it this way." This answer does an excellent job of getting you off the hook. I use it all the time—I blame my board of directors when I have to give a supplier or customer some unpleasant news.

"We don't want our good customers, like you, to pay for the sins of the bad ones. If we don't spell out our policy and changes in it, up front, we'd have to raise our prices, and that wouldn't be fair to you."

"We realize that most people like to know what to expect, and we've been a little lax about that up to now." This answer is right on target. People *do* like to know the rules of doing business with you, and if you've been a little less than forthright about your policies and the consequences for violating them, be human and admit your error and get on with it.

Your Communications Should Serve Your Customers

All your communications, from those designed to sell prospects into becoming customers to those that let a few of them know that you'll sue them if they don't pay, have a common purpose: service to the customers. In collections, serve customers by letting them know precisely the rules for doing business with you. There should be no surprises.

You have to be particularly alert to serving your customers when they become abusive or unreasonable with you. Under those circumstances, you can't indulge in equally abusive comments. For example, if a customer curses when you ask her to pay, you don't curse back. Cursing may make you feel a little better, but it doesn't serve your customer. In Chapter 17, I show you how to handle cursing the way a professional does.

This chapter, plus the insights in Chapter 5, "A Collection Philosophy That Works," comprise most of the key psychological insights and tools you'll need to become a great collector. Another important tool—role playing—is discussed in the next chapter.

Conclusion: As good as these communication strategies are for collecting, there's a bonus—even if your debtor knows what you're doing, these strategies still work.

16

Role Playing, Starring You as the Debtor

If you want to become a great cook, you won't achieve your goal simply by watching "The Frugal Gourmet," Julia Child, Paul Prudhomme, Jeremiah Tower or fifteen other top chefs. They may inspire you, but until you get your own hands on some ingredients and utensils and start chopping, sautéing, roasting, frying, and baking yourself, your dream will be just that—a dream. This is obviously an analogy with collecting. This book and others can give you information about and a point of view on collecting, but you have to parlay your knowledge into a state of confidence and proven results. Role playing is the best method I know for achieving a consistent level of success in collecting.

Many people who are new to collecting are reluctant to enact the role-playing drills because they know they're going to do it wrong, and it's embarrassing to make a public fool of yourself.Other beginners say that role playing isn't real and the situation isn't like confronting a real debtor. I can assure you that the "debtor" comments and your reactions are real enough and no different from what you find in a "real" collection situation.

Doing it "wrong" is an essential step along the way to getting it perfect. For example, look at how movies are made: The producer and director shoot literally 100 times more film than needed for the finished movie we eventually see on the screen. The actors do the takes over and over until they're right. What you don't see in the finished print are the outtakes that wind up on the cutting room floor. Role playing is your cutting room floor and is just as essential.

Rules

The purpose of role playing is to learn how to handle debtor resistance to paying and to be willing to confront that resistance. The purpose is *not* to have a brilliant comeback for every excuse a debtor throws at you. There are four main rules to follow:

1. Only two people get to talk, one the person playing the debtor, the other the collector. Everyone else has to be quiet, which won't be easy. Usually things are said that cause laughter, and others will be tempted to shout out responses or make editorial comments about what the players are saying. Avoid all that.

2. Each player must stay in the role. Say whatever you want to say, but say it as the person you are, either the debtor or the collector. Don't allow phrases such as, "If I were in that situation, I'd say. . . ." or "That happened to me once, and what I said was. . . ." No war stories. Say what you want to say in *this* situation. It's crucial to recognize that each collection situation is *unique*. The words and feelings are never repeated, even by the same two antagonists on two separate but identical-sounding calls.

3. The players don't have to look at each other. There's less stress if they don't and many real collection encounters are on the phone.

4. Nonplaying members of the group must actively listen to determine whether the collector is really communicating with the debtor or simply mouthing scripts or comebacks. The group then offers their observations during the evaluation at the end of each role-playing session.

In a variance of one-on-one role playing, an entire group participates. Form a circle of chairs. Two people begin the exercise—one as the collector, the other as the debtor. Eventually, the debtor or the collector runs out of things to say, at which point someone else in the group takes the chair. Almost always someone will be available to pick up the conversational slack because the nonplaying members of the group aren't under the pressure that the players are; they're freer to listen to what's really going on.

And that's the ultimate goal of the role playing. You want to get to the point where you're so concerned with what's going on with the other person, the debtor, that you don't have to devote much energy to what you're thinking. You don't care about what's going on with you. You're actively listening. You care what's going on with the other person. (You'll better understand what I'm getting at when you actively do your role playing.)

I realize that these words don't mean much because they describe an experience. It's like trying to describe a sneeze. No description compares to actually sneezing yourself. When you sneeze, only then do you really know what a sneeze is all about.

Beginning

The role playing begins with either the debtor or the collector calling first. The collector may know what the situation is all about or may know nothing at all. Let each member of the group write down some problems they've encountered in recent days so that they can role play these problems. Debtor excuses you can role play with include (1) The manager is a friend; (2) I never got the bill; (3) My spouse handles all the bills; (4) You should feel sorry for me; (5) I can pay you when we get paid; (6) I can't pay now/can't pay all/can't pay till next month; (7) Don't you threaten me; (8) Your product was no good; (9) My insurance should take care of this; (10) My attorney says not to pay; (11) The check is in the mail; (12) I'm out of work; (13) I'll send you a dollar a month; (14) Go ahead and sue me.

Tips

During the role playing, the debtor can be easy or hard-nosed, straightforward or evasive, apologetic or profane, or any role she wants to play. Tips for the collector include:

1. Be willing to say no to any unacceptable offers debtors make.
2. Always throw the burden back onto the debtor. If she wants you to talk to her spouse, lawyer, insurance company, or any other party to the bill, tell her to have that person get in touch with you. Clearing up the bill is her problem, not yours.
3. Never lose your cool. If you feel that you might, terminate the conversation.
4. If the debtor is cooperative and makes reasonable offers, you cooperate also. If the debtor isn't reasonable, say what you'll do, and do it.
5. Your job isn't to have the right comeback for every debtor excuse; it's to have a policy and point of view about the bill. Essentially that point of view is, "You got the product or service, debtor, and you haven't paid for it [or all of it] yet, so how do you plan to take care of it?" I may agree with your response or I may not. I don't

know in advance, but I'll let you know when you tell me.

It's vital to recognize that both the debtor and collector make up what they're going to say to each other. Because each player has no idea what the other will say, each one has to make up a response. Every debtor will tell you that when he began the conversation, he had no idea of where it would end and what commitment would be made. Collecting is a dynamic encounter between two people of divergent interests, not a monologue by a robot.

The End

When each role play is finished, the group leader guides the participants through a series of four follow-up questions. First the leader asks the debtor and the collector, "How did you feel going through that?" More often than not, the answer will be what they thought or would have felt, not what they actually felt at the time. The feeling often is anger, discomfort, embarrassment, or other so-called negative feelings. I find that the role player is often reluctant to put herself as well as the other party through that emotional experience, assuming she admits she even had one.

One purpose of the role playing then is to legitimize whatever feelings are being felt. The feelings are neither right nor wrong, nor is it the collector's job to shield the debtor from the debtor's discomfort, as many collectors try to do. On the other hand, some experienced debtors are skilled at feigning upsets to get a collector to back off.

Next, ask the group what collecting "techniques" were used, which could have been used, what seemed to work, what didn't, and why. These questions let everyone become more conscious of all that is happening in a fast-moving verbal encounter.

Third, ask the debtor and the group if the collector was in

communication with the debtor or just mouthing desperate replies. My experience is that most of the group won't know, even though they were there the whole time! Being in communication is difficult to do and to observe because it requires a high level of acknowledgment of the debtor's communications and an awareness of what the debtor is really thinking.

Finally, ask the group to place the debtor on the Spectrum of Debtors. Do they think the debtor will or won't pay? What do they think should happen next? Paradoxically, most of the group will guess correctly as to where on the Spectrum the debtor should be placed, even though they have much more trouble following what is going on during the call.

I observe that even though most people are reluctant to volunteer for role playing, once they get started, it's awfully hard to get them to stop. It becomes fun. In any role playing encounter, if the leader senses that the conversation is going nowhere, it's OK to stop it. Role playing is also valuable for uncovering more clearly what your payment policies are or should be. I recommend regular training and tune-up sessions with all the people involved in your business's credit and collection activities; and role playing should be your main training tool.

_____

Conclusion: Because role playing is used to fine-tune (or wash out) sales trainees and collecting has most of the attributes of selling, role playing sessions for collectors will yield a comparable payoff.

17

Debtor Myths and Games

Debtors' creativity in avoiding or slowing down payment is staggering. Unless you're the creditor to whom the money is owed, you can only smile and admire the thought and energy expended in being irresponsible. Much self-righteousness, denial, and justification comes from debtors who aren't honest. Here's a short list of thoughts debtors use to justify giving you, the creditor, aggravation and collection work:

1. I have a lot of other bills to pay.
2. I'd rather spend it on a vacation.
3. They don't need the money so badly.
4. They should feel sorry for me.
5. I couldn't resist buying it.
6. I'll pay it back some day. Trust me.
7. When I get paid, you'll be the first one I pay back.
8. I expect a big check soon.
9. There's larceny in everyone's heart.

Myths

Certain universal myths that debtors everywhere seem to "know" abound. (1) "As long as I pay you regularly, even $1 a month, there's nothing you can do." This old war story is literally that—a war story. It goes back to the Soldiers and Sailors Relief Act of World War II, which in effect said that if you're making a good faith attempt to pay, even $1 a month, as long as you are a uniformed member of the armed services you can't be required to pay more. Not only is World War II long over, but the act has been struck off the books. It's just awfully hard to convince debtors of that.

(2) "As long as I make regular payments, more than $1 a month, you can't turn me into collection." Wrong. A creditor has the right, at any time, to use a third-party collection service on the unpaid balance and to do it without warning the debtor. In practice, though, a creditor is foolish to do that because if he warns debtors to pay or else go to collection, some of those debtors will pay and the creditor can thereby avoid collection costs.

There's a myth that some angry creditors believe is true: If the debtor doesn't pay, the creditor can attach the debtor's wages, execute on the debtor's bank account, or repossess the debtor's car. At one time a creditor could make a "prejudgment attachment," but not any more. Today you have to get a judgment from a court to repossess, levy, or execute on assets.

Gentle Games

I arbitrarily classify debtor games as gentle or serious games. Let's discuss the gentle games first.

Accusations

Common debtor accusations can include the following:

1. You're harassing me.
2. You're dunning me.
3. You're a moneygrubber.
4. You can't get blood out of a turnip.

These accusations are all false, so simply deny them. "I'm not harassing you." "I'm not dunning you." "I'm not a moneygrubber." "You're not a turnip. You're a business that owes us $250, and you need to tell me how you plan to take care of that."

If you want to take a shot at a debtor who's giving you a particularly bad time, including accusing you of harassment, try this response: "You know, debtor, if you'd paid this bill as agreed, I wouldn't have had to send bills, make phone calls, run up unnecessary expenses, and aggravate myself. Actually, it's you who's harassing me!"

Indignation

"Your prices are unbelievable. What am I doing, paying for the boss's Cadillac?" Any time there's any sign of affluence, such as a new office, a new car, a redecorated customer area, or new stationery, you can expect to be tested. Some jealous debtors will throw the affluence in your face, in an attempt to avoid paying you. I hear about collectors being subjected to this petty annoyance all the time. I don't consider this game anything but a gentle poke in the ribs, which deserves a poke back. For example, if the debtor sees a new fishtank in your waiting area and says, "I guess I'm paying for your new fishtank today," you can respond, in the same spirit, "No, you're paying for just the guppies and the air bubbler, and we really appreciate it. Thanks a lot."

Offensive Tackle

"Why are your prices so high?" This approach is a little trickier. Prices are relative and arbitrary, so a suggestion that yours are "too high" is an attempt to put you on the defensive and avoid talking about how the bill is going to be paid. You can handle this game by responding with a statement such as, "I guess it does seem high. It's amazing how high everything is these days. I remember when gas was twenty cents a gallon, don't you? And the house I live in—I'm glad I bought it twenty years ago, because if I had to buy it today, I couldn't afford it. Now we have to discuss how you plan to take care of this."

You can substitute other examples of how everything seems to go up in price. So, instead of arguing with the debtor, you're agreeing with him but reminding him that the bill has to be paid anyway. All you're really agreeing with is the sentiment. You'd better actually *be* proud of your fees and prices because if you aren't, that feeling will communicate itself to your customers. I promise you that whatever you feel about the reasonableness of your charges will be communicated to the debtor one way or another.

Child Answers Phone—Parents Never Home

This consumer debt problem concerns kids trained by their parents to tell all strange-sounding voices that no one is at home. Of course, this statement coming from a three-, four- or five-year-old is a little surprising considering that someone older should be at home. If you suspect you've reached one of these trained kids (particularly if you hear adult voices in the background) use one of these approaches:

1. (In a stern voice) "Don't you lie to me. You go get your mom right now!" Some kids will respond to a direct order from any authoritative-sounding voice.

2. "Would you please go ask your mom what time she's coming home?" One kid who was told that came back to the phone and said, "My mom said to tell you she's never coming back."

These little ploys work only once with a debtor, when they work at all.

Messages Left on Answering Machines, No Calls Returned

This passive game elicits an active response from you. You have an above-the-line debtor. If a final, certified letter doesn't get a response, bite the bullet.

No Commitment

"I'll try to pay this next week." Mayday! Mayday! The word "try" is a red flag. Your debtor, who sounds so reasonable, has made no commitment whatever. One either does something or one doesn't. Did you ever "try" to lift a glass off a table? No, you either lifted it or you didn't.

Meaningless Promises

The debtor says "I'll send you a payment" or "I'll send you something on this account today." These are meaningless promises. Earlier in this book I asked you to never tell a debtor to send a payment or something on the account because anything you get would then be something or a payment. Similarly, if the debtor offers you a payment, you must refuse it and ask for a specific amount on a specific day. If the debtor doesn't make such a commitment, you make it for him. For example,

Debtor: I'll make a substantial payment today.

You: That's great. I need to know what you mean by substantial.

Debtor: Well, I'm not sure, but I promise to make a big dent in my bill.

You: I appreciate that. What I need is $100 today and the balance in 2 weeks.

Debtor: I'll try. I really will.

You: Don't forget, that's $100 today. Thank you. Goodbye.

This example, shows that you must have the last words, and those words are specific as to how much and when. Does this mean that the debtors will send in the $100 as requested? Certainly not all the time.

But let's look at the alternatives. If you let the debtor have the last word, and she promises nothing specific, in her mind she has committed to nothing so the odds of getting paid are small. On the other hand, your having the last word doesn't necessarily guarantee that you've sold the debtor on your point of view. It does mean that the debtor knows she hasn't sold you on hers. What you've done is produced a condition of uncertainty. Now the debtor doesn't know what will happen if she doesn't send in the $100. We humans don't like rapid change and too much uncertainty. So, rather than find out what will happen if she doesn't send in the $100, most likely in this situation she'll send in the money. Not all debtors will react this way in a similar situation, so you have to play the percentages.

Violation of Agreement

You and the debtor agree to five payments of $50 each. The first payment comes in as promised. The second one is paid on time, but the amount is only $25. You have three choices:(1) Hope the additional $25 will be paid next time, (2) turn the account into collection, (3) call the debtor.

The correct choice is 3. Any time you and the debtor make an agreement, the day the agreement is *not* honored in full, call up your debtor and either: Ask her to keep the agreement, or, if the circumstances have changed or the debtor sells you on some new story, you and the debtor can agree to a new payment plan. What you *don't* do is let the debtor unilaterally, on her own, violate the agreement without an immediate confrontation (OK, let's call it a response) on your part.

Other Forms of Games

There are so many other forms of active and passive resistance to paying that it's too tedious to list them all. I include the debtors who run out of your company yelling "Bill me," the ones who claim to speak no English, those who pay your bill but not the late charge, who pay that $50 bill in pennies—you can see how debtors have unlimited options. In every case, you must sell the debtor on paying. If you fail, place the debtor on the Spectrum and take the appropriate action.

I'll end our "gentle" game section with a situation that will take some courage on your part. Suppose your debtor owes $200 and sends you $5 (which you hadn't agreed to) or some other ridiculous payment. *Send it back*! Crazy? Absurd? No. Do you say, "A bird in the hand is worth two in the bush?" I say a bird in the hand is a big mess. Send back the payment. Your debtor is playing games with you, hoping you'll feel that something is better than nothing. Your debtor is trying to *buy you off*. If you accept the $5, you've been bought.

When you send back the ridiculous payments, a strange thing happens: You usually get more money in return because the debtor knows that the little trick didn't work. When you send back the $5, you enclose a note saying what you will accept. If you don't have the heart to send the $5 back, keep it, but call or send a note saying you're accepting the $5 only as a partial payment on a minimum of so much. In other words, by confronting the small payment game, you're again playing the odds.

Occasionally, you'll return a small payment and your debtor will say, "Fine. You don't want my $5? Then, forget it. I'll send nothing." This can happen, but the odds are small compared to the scenario just described. You've got to be willing to lose a few to win more.

Serious Games

Included in what I arbitrarily call serious games are phones slammed down, crying, screaming, and physical threats. The games are serious because they extract an emotional toll from the collector. These games aren't particularly difficult to place on the Spectrum; they're mostly above the line.

Phone Slammed Down

There isn't much you can do in this situation. This debtor is clearly communicating that he doesn't want to deal with the problem; he gets placed above the line very quickly. You can try the following two approaches to avoid turning this debtor into collection, but neither has much chance of success:

1. Wait a day or two and try again.
2. Call back immediately. When the debtor answers the phone, say that you must have been disconnected. You'll probably get another phone slammed down again.

Cursing

Some debtors will curse you to your face, but most are more likely to do it on the phone. The most professional way to deal with filthy language is this four-step approach:

1. "I'm not willing to talk with you if you use that kind of language."
2. (Cursing continues) "If you keep talking to me like that, I'm going to have to hang up the phone."
3. (More cursing) "I'm going to hang up the phone now."
4. (Still more cursing) Hang up the phone.

The skeptics say, "Sure, that's exactly what they wanted—for you to hang up and buy some more time." Maybe so, but you've given the debtor three chances to think it over, and you can't force the debtor to clean up his language. Once again, you have no guarantee; you're just astutely playing the odds.

Another, slightly more gutsy way of dealing with foul-mouthed debtors was taught to me by an 80-year-old, sweet, grandmotherly woman from a small town. Her first job required her to call some debtors on the phone. One of these debtors shouted some choice obscenities at her. She was only twenty at the time, and she was so unnerved that she put down the phone, walked around the block for a half hour, and asked herself whether she really wanted the job if that was what she had to put up with.

Well, she talked herself into staying because she needed the money. Over the years, she learned how to handle anything. Now, when she calls a debtor who uses foul language, she knows exactly what to do. She lets him mouth off for five or ten seconds. Then she cuts in, saying, "I love it when you talk dirty like that!" She says that stops them every time. Some debtors say, "You do?" This tactic isn't for the faint of heart.

Physical Threats

If the debtor is in your presence and threatens to get physical, end the conversation right away and get away from the debtor.

Screaming

The louder they get, the softer you get. The Bible states it well, "A soft voice turneth away wrath." Your debtor is in the right brain, so reasonable, logical argument is of no use. A little feedback of feelings might help, as in, "I can understand that this is really upsetting you." If the debtor calms down, you might try to resume the logic of why the debt must be paid.

One other approach has been used with good effect. Tell the debtor in a firm voice, either on the phone or face-to-face, *"Stop.* Just stop it." It often works.

Crying

Crying is really unnerving. It may be manipulation by an accomplished actor, or it can be genuine anguish at the despair felt in the situation. Either way, you're likely to be touched. Your usual aplomb will probably be shaken. You have a debtor who, again, is in the right side of the brain—all feeling and very little logic.

It is appropriate to back off now but let the debtor know that the problem isn't going to disappear. You can say, "I'm so sorry this is causing you such distress. Why don't I call you back at another time so we can discuss this?" Whatever part of the debtor's left brain is functioning knows that this is a temporary respite only.

Occasionally, I have employees who want to discuss a problem that is upsetting enough to make them cry. I just stop talking and put the Kleenex in front of them; they get through the crisis quickly.

Never say to someone who's upset or crying that they shouldn't feel that way. This statement only makes the situation worse. Just acknowledge the feeling, and watch it disappear quickly.

Whether the games are gentle or serious, the following truths will help:

1. You can't "control" the conversation. What you can better control is your own reactions to it and your responses to the debtor.

2. You make the rules, and you can refuse to accept the debtor's proposals. (But don't take this to be support for becoming a petty tyrant.)

3. No matter what the debtor does, the underlying reality is that the debt must be taken care of. That is your point of view; how you express it is of secondary importance.

———

Conclusion: Debtor games are no joke.

18

Collection Problems, Stalls, Excuses

⎯⎯⎯⎯⎯

This chapter is a continuation of the previous one in that it deals with debtor resistance. The focus here is on the specific, classic excuses and the more effective responses. The responses are initial responses, because you've no idea what hidden agenda may be going on or where the conversation will veer. To reiterate a point made in Chapter 16, on role playing, there's no such thing as a script you can follow for the infinite variety of excuses debtors can create.

The examples in this chapter suggest good conversational counters and the point of view that underlies them. If you, the credit grantor, make a mistake, apologize and correct it immediately and personally. If the money is owed, you expect the debtor to take care of it, in full. If the debtor refuses to pay it all in full now, you'll be prepared to negotiate. If you get to the point where you feel no more can be gotten, you'll quit and bite the bullet.

"I Never Got Your Bill."

When the debtor offers you this stall, you should immediately come back with, "What is your current address?" If the address the debtor gives is different from the one that you have on record, you should take down the new address and respond, "I'll have it sent right out to your new address. Do you plan to handle payment by check or credit card?"

If the address is the same, respond with, "That's the address we used. I'll send another bill today. Do you plan to take care of it when you receive it?" Your responses are closing off debtor escape routes. Your next comment or action will depend on how cooperative or evasive your debtor is.

"Your Computer Must Be Fouled Up. We Never Bought Any of This Stuff."

You should reply by asking the name of the company, for example, "Is this the Great American Electric Company at 23 Nordhoff Drive?" If the person replies that it is, you say, "Well, Jay Berger ordered them October 5 and we delivered them."If the person replies that you've reached the wrong address, reply, "Sorry, our mistake. What phone number is this, please?"

"May I Tell Him What This Is About?" (Debtor's Secretary Is an Efficient Call Screener)

You should tell the secretary why you're calling: "It's about a large unpaid bill owed to us." If the secretary says,"I'll transfer you to our accounts payable department,"respond with, "I've already talked with them, and we got nowhere. Please tell your boss that he needs to call me today at 687-9456, or this matter is out of my hands."

"I Have Other Bills to Pay."

This is a common excuse. We all have bills to pay, so logically reply, "This is one of your bills and must be paid in full now. What we need to do is discuss how you plan to do this.

"I Can't Pay You Anything Now."

Most people can pay something, so respond with one of two questions (1) "Are you receiving social security? Unemployment compensation? Welfare?" (If the debtor answers no to all three questions, you know you have a liar.) (2) "Are you paying your house payment? Your car payment? Your utilities?" If the debtor answers no again, you probably have a liar. If the debtor answers yes, tell the debtor that your bill has to be paid also and begin the negotiation.

"Sue Me? Get in Line, Buddy."

Just say, "Thank you. Goodbye." There's not much to discuss here. Go ahead and sue.

"How Can You Ask an Old Lady Like Me to Pay?"

Believe me, the debtor's heart *won't* break if you tell her: "I'm truly sorry if this is causing you distress, and I wish I didn't have to call you, but you do owe $185 and you do need to take care of it now."

"The Check Is in the Mail."

To counter this lame cliché, say, "Great. What's the check number? When was it sent? In what amount? To whom? How was it sent?"

"I Can Send You $5 a Month."

On a large bill you have to say, "On your $500 bill we just can't accept that." If the debtor then says, "I swear that's all I can pay," you respond with, "If you'll come into our office and fill out a statement of income and expenses, I may be able to grant you an extension on this, but that's the only way I can do it." If the debtor does come in and provide the information, you have a sign of debtor responsibility and can cooperate. If the debtor refuses, you're better off letting a third party, such as a collection agency, try to reason with the debtor.

"My Husband Handles All the Bills."

Handle this ploy by hinting that you'll contact the husband at work, if necessary: "I'm sure he doesn't want to be bothered at work. Please have him call me tomorrow, so we can get this cleared up. Tell him it's an urgent matter that must be dealt with now. Thank you."

"We Can Pay You When Our Customers Pay Us."

This is a very common stall. You may be tempted to ask how they can afford to pay the staff, but instead you say, "I wish we could do business with you like that, but I have a better idea. I'm going to recommend some places you can borrow from so you can pay this, and you can choose which one is best for you."

I'm not suggesting that all these responses will squelch all debtor resistance. We have no idea how the dialogue will develop. I want to restate a key objective in your communications: to bring a dash of reality to the debtor and see to what degree they accept it so that you can determine your next comment or next step.

"I'm Not Working Now."

An understanding response is: "I'm really sorry to hear that. When did that happen? What are your prospects? Where is your wife working? Let's discuss some other sources of money to take care of this bill and perhaps some of your other ones."

"We Went With Another Company. Why Should We Have to Pay for Your Project Design?"

If you respond with, "Do you remember my telling you that you'd have to pay for the design work regardless of who got the construction work?", you're on weak bargaining grounds. Any agreement should have been in writing. Your oral agreement may stand up in court, if this case goes there, but I wouldn't count on it.

"My Insurance Will Cover This."

Tell the debtor that "Your insurance may cover as much as 80 percent, but we never know. Besides, we don't wait for insurance to pay. If you'll send 30 percent of the bill now, we'd be willing to wait thirty days for the insurance money. If there's an overpayment, we'll refund the balance to you immediately. If we don't get paid in thirty days, we'll look to you for payment."

"Our Attorney Is Handling This."

You may come back immediately with, "Please have your attorney contact us within 24 hours." However, experienced collectors will recognize this dialogue as too simplistic. The debtor may then say the attorney is on vacation for a month, the attorney may try to stonewall you, or the attorney may never get back to you, and more. If the attorney doesn't respond, send a certified letter that states: "Unless we hear from you within 48 hours, we will assume you are no longer the attorney of record." That usually gets a response.

"You Leeches Better Stop Calling Me."

Respond with, "I can understand that you're upset about this. The only reason I'm calling is that you haven't paid the bill. I promise you this is the last call. Why don't we discuss this calmly so I don't have to turn it into collection?"

"No Speak English."

You have a problem here. If no one does speak English, you can't discuss the bill. Maybe you can guess the language spoken and send a message in the mail in that language. Perhaps you can ask for an English-speaking relative or neighbor. Some collectors have smoked out a fake by distinctly pronouncing the word "collection" into the phone, or, if the bill is large enough, you may be able to get someone who speaks the language to talk to the debtor. It's curious that when someone wants to buy something, language is not as much of a barrier as when the time comes to pay for it.

"I'm Divorced. Call Harry. The Judge Said He's Responsible. I Have a Court Order That Proves It."

You usually have a selling job to do when divorce intrudes on an unpaid bill. If the wife incurred the debt, she'll find it convenient to absolve herself of all responsibilities. Tell her that "This bill was incurred before the divorce [assuming that is so], so you're as responsible as your ex-husband. The court order is between you and him; we are not party to it. We'll be happy to bill Harry as a courtesy, but if he does not pay this within ten days, we will look to you for the full amount."

"I Need an Extension on This."

Be specific in your reply: "How much time do you need to clear this in full?", or "Before we can grant an extension, you must come in and discuss your exact financial situation. Besides, we may be able to help you in ways you weren't aware of."

"Your Product Is No Good."

Merely say, "We stand 100 percent behind our product. Please return it and we will send you another one, and the balance of $200 is due at this time." We're into policy issues now. What do you do if the customers claim that they don't want the product, it isn't what they expected, it's too expensive, they've changed their mind, the product has since gone on sale, or whatever? Basically, your policy should include a willingness to accommodate any reasonable customer request, but declare that products kept, or services received, must be paid for. A few companies will knowingly let customers rip them off with a no-questions-asked return policy because they make more profitable sales than the small losses they accept in the bargain.

"I'm Bankrupt."

Ask, "When did that happen? Please send me a copy of the bankruptcy notice." I'll discuss bankruptcy in more detail in the next chapter. If your debt was incurred prior to the bankruptcy, you may be out of luck in collecting and you may not pursue the debtor further. Go on to another account.

"I'll Send You Something on This Soon."

You already know how to handle this stall, based on our previous discussion: "I appreciate that, and what I need to know is exactly what you plan to send and when." Now, you're off and running in the negotiation.

"I'm Not Paying. Period."

You have to love a debtor like this because he's so straightforward; he tells you up front that you have a big problem, which saved you from wasting time fishing for the bad news. Try this: "Thank you for being so honest with me. Would you tell me why you say that?" The debtor's response tells you whether you have someone you can reason and negotiate with or an intransigent debtor who helps you make an easy decision to bring in a third party, professional collector.

"I Just Can't Pay It All Now."

Your debtor is asking you to negotiate, so go ahead. "We can accept half now and a post-dated check for the balance sent with it." May the best salesperson win.

"I'm Not the Person Who Owes This. That's My Dad, John B. Martin."

Do *not* say, "Oops, sorry. Where can I reach him?" This really could be John B. Martin who's playing a game, pretending to be someone else. Whatever happens next will tell the story; John B. emerges and pays, John B. calls back and won't pay, there is no John B., or the debtor is actually John B. but won't admit it. The game playing can become tiresome, but you can become quicker at sensing deception.

"My Filling Fell Out."

Trying to somehow blame you won't work. Respond with, "That was a *temporary* filling. It was never intended to last for years. You were supposed to return Friday so the doctor could put in a permanent filling."

Conclusion: When you're in the mood for it, you can feel admiration for debtors' inventiveness. When you're sick of the game playing, you may wish that the energy that goes into excuses would be redirected to getting the money to pay you.

19

Nitty–Gritty Details

In collecting, the correct use of psychology and the right selling techniques will give you most of your successes. You'll also need some left-brain information about the facts and procedures for the many technical issues you'll encounter. This chapter enumerates key technical points to be aware of in collection, with this caveat:

> Because many of the facts vary by state, and I don't want to present pages of charts, before incorporating *any* of this information in this chapter, *check with your business attorney.*

Bankruptcy

Bankruptcies are on the rise, particularly personal bankruptcies. Going bankrupt used to be considered shameful, a sign of failure, but in recent years it has gained a status closer to a badge of honor.

Books proclaim the virtue of getting even with creditors through bankruptcy and present the information necessary for doing it. We can't do anything about the free flow of information in this country, so let's look at what to do if your debtor does declare bankruptcy. Three main types of bankruptcy may affect your business: liquidation, wage earner's plan, and business and farm reorganization.

Chapter 7: Liquidation Bankruptcy

This type is the biggest trouble for you because you usually wind up with nothing. Once you're on notice of the filing, you can't do anything to try to collect the debt: no contacts by phone, letter, or in person. If you filed suit, you must dismiss the suit. If you've already obtained judgment against the debtor, you can't undertake any legal process to attempt recovery; if you do, you'll be in contempt of court. Your bargaining position is zero.

You'll receive a notice of bankruptcy that tells you if your debtor has any assets that can be sold to pay off creditors. If you have a debt secured by physical assets, such as a house or a car, your chances of getting money are considerably better than if you have an unsecured debt. Fill out the bankruptcy form, but don't hold your breath waiting for a shower of money.

Chapter 13: Wage Earner's Plan

This part of the bankruptcy laws is designed to help individual consumer debtors. With this program, you, the creditor, are likely to get a portion of your debt paid, usually within three to five years. All you have to do is fill out the form you'll receive and cease all further debtor contact. You'll be invited to a meeting of creditors, which is normally a waste of time.

Other Chapters: Business and Farm Reorganization

A number of other chapters allow businesses, farms, and

other types of organizations that file for bankruptcy to handle their debts under court protection. Consult your attorney.

Bad Checks

A few years ago, the "experts" predicted that we were on the verge of a checkless and paperless society. In spite of electronic fund transfers and data transfers, today we have more checks than ever as well as more computer paper. Imagine what mountains of paper we'd be buried under without the electronic assistance!

A growing number of companies specialize in protection and guarantees, for a fee, against bad checks. Businesses that buy these services don't always use them as they should. And for checks under a certain amount, such as $50, the services aren't economical at all. So we're left with the continuing problem of bad checks. The solution depends on what kind of bad check you have—no account, closed account, or insufficient funds:

1. No account—The check is a fraud.
2. Closed account—The bank has closed the account, probably because the consumer has been overdrawing. Treat it like an insufficient fund check.
3. Insufficient funds (NSF)—There's not enough money in the account to pay the check. Bringing criminal action, although tempting, is usually a waste of time and may slow the recovery of your money. Don't threaten your debtor with criminal action if he doesn't pay; the threat may be considered blackmail under state criminal statutes and will probably be defined as harassment.

Many states have check collection statutes that allow you to recover your costs for collecting NSF checks. You also may be allowed to add additional charges if collection actions are required and if you post a notice in your business warning any potential passer of a bad check about the consequences of such action. Simple collection actions to take with an NSF check are:

1. Call the bank to see if the check is now good.
2. Call the debtor and ask for a new, good check or for money to be deposited into the account.
3. Contact the debtor's bank and ask them for Enforced Collection, which means that your check is held in a special category and the next money deposited to the debtor's account goes to you. Banks have varying procedures for this technique, so call your bank to find out what to do.

Deceased Debtor

In most states, if a deceased debtor has a surviving spouse, you can attempt collection from that spouse, who's as legally liable as the deceased. If there is no spouse, there usually is an estate, normally announced in the public records section of the local newspaper. File a claim against the estate, obtain a form from the court, fill it out, and attach a copy of the document, such as an itemized statement, that gives proof of the money owed to you. You must file your claim promptly—usually within ninety days of death—or you forever lose all ability to recover from the estate.

Once the claim has been properly filled out and filed, if the deceased has assets, you get paid before any assets are distributed to the heirs. Relatives of the deceased, such as brothers, sisters, and adult children are under no legal obligation to pay the deceased person's debts, but they may feel morally bound to do so. You can ask them to pay, but you have to back off if they decline.

Attorneys

The word "attorney" evokes strong thoughts and feelings in people, mostly negative. As Shakespeare said, when contemplating how to organize a better future, "First, shoot all the attorneys." Another of my favorite quotations is from G. B. Shaw, the quintessential antiestablishmentarian, who observed, "All professions are a conspiracy against the laity."

You may want *your* attorney to be the meanest, most intimidating person you can find. In business transactions, attorneys have been known to intimidate, if they can get away with it. If your customer is an attorney, be on guard. Some businesses won't even do business with a person known to be an attorney, or, if they do, they have the attorney sign a document that certifies the obligation to pay. If your debtor retains an attorney to handle the debt, you may face the following problems.

Debtor Claims Attorney Told Him Not to Pay Anything

Whether or not the attorney actually said that, you may have an above-the-line debtor. Sometimes, talking to the attorney will get you closer to getting paid if the attorney is more rational than the debtor.

Even though an attorney is handling the debt, it's the debtor who's responsible for the bill and you can, if necessary, sue for your money. Some debtors hang on to a self-induced fantasy that having an attorney absolves them of having to pay the bill.

Debtor Tells You to Deal with Attorney But Attorney Won't Return Calls

This condition is common; the attorney hopes you'll go away. If you're ignored one or two times, do as I suggested in

Chapter 18: Send a certified letter that states, "Unless we hear from you within 48 hours, we will assume you are no longer the attorney of record."That usually works; if it doesn't, go after your debtor directly.

Attorney Stalls You or Makes a Ridiculous Offer

Show no mercy. Demand payment. Negotiate as though your survival depended on the outcome. Don't accept any offer that you would have turned down from the debtor.

The attorney is an ordinary human being. If she spouts legal jargon, insist that it be put into plain English. If you feel that you're being intimidated, inform the attorney of that feeling, state that you won't be intimidated, and that you are within your rights to sue for the full balance immediately, plus costs and filing fees.

If the size of the account justifies it, refer the account to your attorney for handling. Document the essence of the conversation carefully.

Attorney Offers a Lien or Attorney Protection Letter

If a third party, such as an insurance company, may be judged liable to pay, the attorney for the debtor is likely to ask you to wait for your money until the case comes to trial and is decided. In the meantime, the attorney will "protect" you with a document that promises to pay you after trial.

Several problems ensue with this safe-sounding idea. The case will undoubtedly take years to come to trial. Your debtor may not win. If the debtor does win, the award may not be enough to satisfy all claims and pay the attorney. The attorney may never notify you of the case settling. The attorney may refuse to pay you. The money may be paid direct to the debtor, who refuses to pay you or denies he got it.

All these horror stories happen, and happen far more frequently than you might imagine, which is why I'm very reluctant to agree to an attorney's lien or a protection letter—I want the bill paid now. You don't have any obligation to wait for your money. If you do, that's a courtesy on your part as well as a big risk.

If you do accept the lien, you want the debtor, as well as the attorney, to sign for the obligation. In a few sections of the country, an attorney lien is as good as gold. Check with other creditors in your field, and be very cautious.

Debtor's Attorney Talks About Suing You for Some Defect in Your Product or Service— Let Your Attorney Take Over

One effective way of dealing with a debtor's attorney is to cater to their sense of importance and superior legal knowledge. Say, "I realize that you're an expert in the law, and I can't possibly win in any debate with you; I'd be out of my league." A little groveling at this time is a good ploy. Then go on to say that you're in a position to accept payment on the account but that any other conversation is out of your hands. See how forthcoming the attorney is, and take action accordingly.

Finance Charge

To repeat the warning at the beginning of the chapter, check all these legal sounding paragraphs with your attorney. This section provides a direction and a point of view if you aren't now using a finance charge on unpaid bills.

Philosophically speaking, if you add a finance charge (also called interest, service charge, carrying charge, etc.), your bill will be paid faster. Without it, time is on the debtor's side; it costs her nothing to delay payment. There's actually a disincentive to pay because an unpaid bill earns interest for the debtor.

To reduce the negative incentive, you make the debtor pay for sitting on your money. Interest, service charge, carrying charge, or any other charge to your debtor, brought about in connection with the extension of credit, and referred to in the Federal Truth-in-Lending Act as a finance charge, is subject to all the rules of the act and, above all, must be properly disclosed. Your attorney will advise you about how to disclose and the maximum you can charge. Disclosure normally means that you inform every debtor of the finance charges, in writing, normally by including it on each statement. It does *not* mean that the debtor has to sign something as proof he was informed.

A finance charge is usually expressed as a percentage of the total amount due. You can also use a similar device called a rebilling charge, which is a flat charge, such as $2 a month. Companies that use a flat rebilling charge claim that it has three advantages over a percentage:

1. Easier to calculate. Of course, if you have a computer, percentages are no trouble to compute.
2. Seems fairer to the debtors because you aren't charging more for a big bill than a small one. That is, it isn't a punitive device, just fair compensation for your added billing costs.
3. A finance charge or a rebilling charge enables you to be flexible as to how you enforce it, depending on your internal payment policy. Remember that this is the part of your policy that debtors don't see. You can

    Waive the charge, one time, on a selective basis. Say to the debtor, "This is the first time you haven't paid on time, so we won't charge you extra *this time.*"

    Tell the debtor that the account is now two months old, which means an added $10, but if he pays it all now, you'll go to bat to get that $10 cut in half.

    Go ahead and charge the full amount as planned.

You have to impose the charge equally on everyone, but

you may selectively waive it (just as you can write off the principal sum, for any reason).

Another tool that helps get more money is a discount for payment at the time the product or service is provided. You can offer a discount up to 5 percent, to induce payment by cash, check, or credit card, at the time of providing the product or service. This discount won't constitute a finance charge under the Federal Truth-in-Lending Act if you offer and disclose it to all customers.

Statute of Limitations

You shouldn't have too many encounters with your state's statute because your bills hopefully will be paid up or written off beforehand. Two to ten years is normally the amount of time you have to go after your debtors. After that, it's as though they went bankrupt in that you can't pursue the debt. Five factors affect the statute:

1. A payment usually extends the statute. If you have a four-year limitation and your debtor makes a payment in the second year, the limitation is extended four more years.

2. Leaving the state where the debt occurred normally suspends the statute until the debtor returns, if she does.

3. Signing a written instrument in evidence of the debt, such as a promissory note signed at the time the product or service is delivered, often creates a new limitation of greater length than that of a straight debt. For example, if the normal limit is four years, a written instrument can extend it to eight or ten years.

4. If an instrument is signed *after* the debt has been incurred, the statute is normally extended. For example, the statute provides for eight years. In the seventh year the debtor signs a written acknowledgment. You get another eight years or even longer, to collect.

5. If you file a civil suit to collect, you extend the statute as long as ten to twenty years, if you win the suit.

Promissory Note

You may tell the debtor that you can extend credit if she signs a promissory note. The note gives you several advantages:

1. Helps induce in a debtor a sense of legitimacy together with urgency for payment.
2. Eliminates legal defenses to the indebtedness. Once the note is signed, it's difficult or impossible for a debtor to produce reasons why the debt isn't owed.
3. Allows you to assess a legal rate of interest.
4. If the debtor defaults and a provision for that action is in the document, you can add attorney fees to the principal sum.

When you draft a note or charge interest, you will comply with the Federal Truth-in-Lending Act by including the (1) principal amount; (2) finance charge, if any; (3) annual percentage rate of interest; (4) payment schedule—number and amount of payments; and (5) total payments. Your attorney can easily create a document that complies with the law. You can also buy an acceptable form at a stationery store.

Separation and Divorce

We're into a messy area here, which isn't surprising, given the high level of emotionalism that usually accompanies these events. When a divorce occurs, you can expect to hear two comments from your debtor:

1. My spouse handles all the bills.
2. The court order says my spouse is responsible.

The confusion is understandable. The court order is between the two parties and doesn't refer to any creditors of either spouse. The court order may, for example, require the ex-husband to pay the ex-wife child support and other expenses. It's highly unlikely that the order will specifically say that the ex must pay your specific bill.

If a bill is a necessity of life, such as a medical bill, both parties are liable for a debt incurred prior to a formal separation or dissolution of marriage. Your business may or may not be considered a necessity of life. Ask your attorney. If a divorced debtor claims that you have to pursue the ex-spouse for the money, explain that you'll do it as a courtesy but that if the debt isn't paid in thirty days, you'll look to the person you're talking with for payment in full and that you expect that person to sign an agreement to that effect. If the debtor refuses, you have good evidence of an above-the-line debtor, one living in a fantasy world, where the denial mechanism is stronger than the sense of responsibility.

When you encounter a divorce, ask for the name of the attorney who represents the debtor. The attorney may give information more clearly than the debtor or may be able to talk sense to the client about the advisability of paying.

Miscellaneous

Problems involving Workers Compensation claims and collecting from minors are discussed in Chapter 22. The use of, and the problems associated with, builders liens is so complex that a book on that subject alone would be more appropriate.If I left anything out, check with your attorney.

Conclusion: The other guy's attorney may be an SOB. Yours can save your hide. Pick a good one and listen up.

20

Harassment—It's Not Really Necessary

As you're attempting to collect on the phone, the debtor shouts, in obvious anger, "You can't harass me! I know my rights. I'm going to call my attorney." Whoops. Now what do you do? Have you inadvertently done or said something that might possibly be interpreted as harassment? If you aren't sure, the prudent thing to do is back off.

But there's no point backing off just because you aren't sure what harassment is. In this chapter, you find out. I spell out, in mind-numbing detail, the rules of the Federal Fair Debt Collection Practices Act (FDCPA) as enacted by the U.S. Congress and interpreted by the Federal Trade Commission (FTC). The FDCPA applies only to collection agencies and attorneys doing collection work for others; it does *not* apply to your business.

There are good reasons for focusing on the federal law. First, the states all have harassment legislation that in many cases is similar to the federal law. Second, if you follow the FDCPA, which is about as tough as it gets, you'll know with sufficient certainty that you're not violating any laws. So, even if a debtor accuses you of harassment, you can be content in knowing that you aren't guilty. You may not be able to convince the debtor, but that's another matter. Right now, I want to suggest that you don't back off prematurely or, for that matter, actually commit an act of harassment out of ignorance.

As you read the specifics of the act, it will become increasingly obvious that you need only do what you say, say and do only what you can— no bluffing, and no threatening. It's practically like the Golden Rule: Do Unto Others As You Would Have Them Do Unto You.

These rules came about because of abuses by a small number of vindictive, unprofessional, out-of-control collectors, the kind who'd make threats vicious enough to curdle the blood of most case-hardened gang enforcers. It's also true that some debtors commit unprovoked acts to tempt retribution from the most gentle of us—acts such as sending in a $100 payment in pennies—COD; enclosing fecal matter instead of payment; calling the collector horrible names; threating the collector; and many more. Unfortunately, getting even isn't allowed; the normal collector can think about it, but he or she just can't do it.

Commonly Asked Questions About FDCPA

When Can You Call a Debtor at Home

You can call at any time convenient for the debtor, which is normally from 8:00 A.M. to 9:00 P.M. in the debtor's time zone. This definition needs further analysis.

Suppose your debtor works the swing shift, also called the second shift, or the lobster shift, as they call it in New England, which may be the third shift. If you call your debtor at 2:00 P.M. a fine time for most people, she or he may be sleeping. The first time you call at 2:00 P.M and she's sleeping isn't harassment if you didn't know that was a bad time to call.

But the next time you call at or around 2:00 P.M. and she's sleeping is harassment because you did know or should have known that your debtor usually sleeps at that time.

How should you have known? By writing it down the first time you called. *Always* record all your communications. As for concern about time zones, most of your debtors will be in your own time zone, or you may live close to the intersection of two of them. Just be sure to add or subtract enough hours to compensate for the difference, if any.

Can You Call a Debtor on the Job?

Some collectors are confused about this point, so let's take it a step at a time. First, if you're dealing with a commercial debt, you can talk to anyone at the business about the bill. With a consumer debt, the rules are much more circumscribed.

You *may* call a consumer debtor on the job, and you don't have to call at home first either, although I recommend that you do. Calling on the job is inherently more stressful to a debtor, and you don't need to go out of your way to help create resistance and stress when you'd be better off if you tried at home first.

But suppose you do call the debtor on the job, only she doesn't answer—a coworker or a supervisor does. You can't tell them what you're calling about, and you can't say that it's some kind of emergency (unless it is) as an inducement to get them to bring your debtor to the phone. What you can say is that it's personal or personal business and then leave your name and phone number. You can also leave the name of the company you're calling from unless that name would provide information that could cause your debtor to lose her job. For example, if you're calling from the Harris County Hospital for the Mentally Deranged, keep that fact to yourself.

Businesses that provide products or services such as mental health treatment, substance abuse treatment, and the like are all forbidden by their attorneys to leave that information with anyone but the debtor. Some female collectors, calling either at the job or at home, in a sexy voice leave their first name and a phone number if they don't get the debtor himself. This ploy gets a response, but it's a no-no, on the grounds that it misrepresents the nature of the call.

Suppose you call a debtor on the job and the debtor does answer or is brought to the phone but says, "Don't you ever call me here again." You can't call again, and he doesn't have to put that in writing either. *You* put it in writing on your collection call notes. But this demand by the debtor doesn't end the call. You respond with, "Fine, Mr. Debtor, I won't call you here on the job, as you request, but I can't reach you at your home phone either. All I get is a recording, and you never return the call. You've also ignored the mail we've sent on this. Therefore, what we have to do is discuss on *this* phone call how you plan to take care of this bill, in a way that will work for both of us, or I have no choice but to place the account in our collection agency, which I'd prefer not to do. We really like to work things out directly with our customers one on one, but if you're unwilling to do that, I have no choice, so won't you please tell me how you plan to pay this so I don't have to turn the account into collection?"

You've given a clear choice, you've sugarcoated your promise to use a collection agency, and you've been forthcoming about all you've done up to this point to communicate with the debtor. If this fails, you can be content in turning the account into collection, knowing that you're making a business decision, and not merely trying to get even.

How Often Can You Call?

The answer is: not too often. To be more specific, whether or not harassment exists is ultimately determined by a jury of people such as you and I. Suppose we're on a jury and learn that a collector has called a debtor once a month. Is that considered too often? Most people don't consider it so.

Is calling once a week too often? Again, most people don't think so. On the other hand, a collector calling every hour on the hour isn't generally considered reasonable. The tactic sounds more like the act of a vindictive person trying to get some satisfaction for being ignored.

The difficulty of defining how often is too often brings to mind a well-known story attributed to Supreme Court Justice Lewis Powell, who was asked to give a definition of pornography. He said, "I can't define it, but I know it when I see it." Calling too often is pretty much like that, wouldn't you agree?

Who Can You Communicate With About the Bill?

With a commercial bill, you can communicate with anyone in the debtor company. With a consumer bill, you can talk or write to the debtor, the attorney who's handling the matter, and, in many states, the spouse. The implications of this ruling include:

1. You can't send a postcard about the debt through the mail because the post office personnel could read about it.

2. You can't have the words "Past Due" on the envelope. You can't put anything on an envelope that indicates the contents are about money owed. ·

3. You have to be careful with answering machines. Always assume that Melvin Belli is listening in and will be delighted to sue you for allowing him to hear what you're calling about. Mel Belli, also known as the King of Torts, is the fellow who was among the first to fly to Bhopal, India, when Union Carbide's plant accident killed and injured so many people. You never know who'll be standing by when the message is played. You should say something like, "This is Marty Anderson calling from Hi-Top Shoe Company about an important matter. Will you please call me right back between 8 and 4:30? Thank you." (It's OK to use words like "urgent" and "important" in your message.)

FDCPA Rules of Harassment

Prohibited Communication With a Consumer Debtor

Without the consumer's prior consent, a debt collector may not communicate with a consumer in connection with the collection of any debt:

- At any unusual time or place.
- At any time or place that is "inconvenient."
- Other than between the hours of 8:00 A.M. and 9:00 P.M. at the debtor location (unless specific circumstances indicate that other times are neither unusual nor inconvenient).
- If the debt collector knows the debtor is represented by an attorney and the name and address of the attorney are either available or readily ascertainable, all communication must take place with the attorney unless the attorney indicates that she or he does not represent the debtor in connection with collection of the debt in question.
- At the debtor's place of employment (unless permitted by the employer).
- If the consumer gives the debt collector written notice that he refuses to pay the debt or wishes the debt collector to stop all communications, except to (1) inform the consumer that debt collection efforts are being terminated, (2) notify consumer that debt collector or creditor may seek certain remedies that the credit grantor normally takes, (3) tell the debtor that the credit grantor intends to initiate a specific remedy.

Communication With Third Parties: Skiptracing

A debt collector may contact third parties to acquire information about locating a missing debtor subject to the following guidelines:

- Collector may not state or infer that the debtor owes a debt.
- Collector may not contact a third party more than once unless it is necessary to do so to obtain complete location information.
- Collector may not place language or symbols on mail to third persons indicating that the mail relates to debt collection.
- Collector may not continue to contact third parties after learning the name and address of the consumer's attorney, unless the attorney fails to respond to the collector's communication.
- Collector, if asked, may not let a third party know the collector is calling about indebtedness; the collector may only respond that the matter concerns "personal business."

Communication With Third Parties: Debt Collection

Without the prior consent of the debtor given directly to the collector, or the express permission of a court of competent jurisdiction, a collector may communicate about indebtedness only with the debtor, the debtor's spouse if responsible (see section on Who's Responsible); a consumer reporting agency, and the attorney representing the debtor.

- If directed to do so, a collector must deal with a debtor's attorney (and may not communicate with the debtor) unless the attorney doesn't respond to the collector's communication after a reasonable period of time.
- If given direct oral or written permission by the debtor, the collector may discuss the debt with any other third party.

Harassment and Abuse

Debt collectors may not resort to harassment or abusive tactics. The FDCPA lists conduct that's absolutely prohibited:

- Use or threat of violence that could harm the person, property, or reputation of any individual.
- Use of obscene, profane or abusive language.
- Publications of a list of consumers who allegedly don't pay their debts.
- Making anonymous telephone calls to the debtor.
- Making continuous or repeated telephone calls to the debtor.

Minors

In most states, a minor is a person under the age of eighteen. An emancipated minor is a person, usually between the ages of fifteen and eighteen who is, by court decree, considered an adult and therefore responsible for the debts they incur. When dealing with minors,

- You're prohibited from talking to minors about bills. You must talk to the parent or guarantor.
- If the debtor is over eighteen, you're prohibited from talking to the parents unless they've guaranteed the debt.
- If the debtor is over eighteen but covered by the parent's insurance, you can talk to the parents and the insurance company about their respective portions of the bill.

False or Misleading Representations

A collector may not use any false, deceptive, or misleading representation in connection with the collection of a debt. Although not limited to these restrictions, the following practices are prohibited:

1. The false representation that the collector is bonded (or vouched for) by the United States, or any state—including the use of a badge, uniform, or facsimile thereof.

2. A false representation of

   The character, amount, or legal status of any debt;

   Any services rendered or compensation that may be lawfully received by a collector for the collection of a debt.

3. False impression that any individual is an attorney or that any communication is from an attorney.

4. Representation that nonpayment of any debt will result in imprisonment or seizure, garnishment, or sale of any property or wages of any person, unless such action is lawful and the collector (or credit client) intends to take such action.

5. Threat to take any action that can't be taken legally or that isn't intended to be taken. (A very strict interpretation of this rule would prevent you from stating to a debtor that you're going to turn the account into collection in three days and you then wait, say, ten days.)

6. False representation or implication that the interest in the debt might be sold, referred, or transferred and that such action may cause the debtor to lose claim or defense to payment of the debt or subject to any practice prohibited by the law.

7. False representation that the debtor committed a crime or other conduct to disgrace the debtor.

8. Communicating or threatening to communicate to any person credit information that should be known to be false, including failure to communicate that a disputed debt is disputed.

9. Use or distribution of any form or document that simulates or falsely represents that it's authorized, issued or approved by any court, official, or agency of the

United States or any state, or which creates any false impression as to its source, authorization, or approval.

10. False representation or deceptive means used to collect or attempt to collect a debt or obtain information about a debtor.

11. Except as provided under the skiptracing section of the law, failure to disclose clearly in all communications to collect a debt or obtain information about a consumer (other than location information) that the collector is attempting to collect a debt and that information obtained will be used for that purpose.

12. False representation that the accounts have been turned over to third-party purchasers for value.

13. False representation or implication that documents are legal process.

14. Use of any business, company, or organization name other than the true name of the collection service (refers to collection agencies). *Note*: A collector may use a "business" or desk name or personal name because the law is silent regarding the use of aliases.

15. False representation or implication that documents aren't legal process forms or don't require action by the consumer (when in actual fact they are).

16. False representation or implication that a debt collector operates or is employed by a consumer reporting agency.

Unfair Practices

A collector may not use unconscionable means to collect or to attempt to collect any debt. Although not limited to these restrictions the following practices are prohibited:

1. Collection of any amount (including any interest, fee, charge, or expense incidental to the principal obliga-

tion) unless such amount is expressly authorized by the agreement creating the debt or permitted by law.

2. Acceptance by a collector from any person of a check (or other payment instrument) postdated by more than five (5) days unless such person is notified in writing of the collector's intent to deposit such check (or instrument) not more than ten (10) nor less than three (3) business days prior to such deposit.

3. Solicitation of a postdated check (or other instrument) by a collector for the purpose of threatening or instituting criminal prosecution.

4. Depositing or threatening to deposit any postdated check (or other instruments) prior to the date on such check (or instruments).

5. Causing charges to be made to any person by concealing the true nature of a communication. Such charges include but are not limited to collect telephone calls and telegram fees.

6. Taking or threatening to take any nonjudicial action to dispossess or disable property if there's no right to possession of the property claimed as collateral through an enforceable security interest; or if there's no present intention to take possession of the property; or if the property is exempt by law from dispossession or disablement.

7. Communicating with a debtor by postcard regarding a debt.

8. Using any symbol or language other than the collection service's (or debt collector's) address on any envelope when communicating with the debtor by mail or by telegram, except that you can use your business name if the name doesn't indicate that you're in the collection business. This restriction doesn't prohibit the use of a company name that doesn't directly indicate that it's a

collection service company, nor does it prohibit the use of the company name followed by the address.

If you read all those rules and your eyes glazed over a bit, you're in good company. The U.S. Congress, bless 'em, tried to leave no loopholes.

Inadvertent Harassment

You need to know the odds of getting in trouble if you mistakenly do something that's an act of harassment. The probability is that nothing will happen unless (1) you have a very angry debtor who wants to get even and reports you to the FTC or to state authorities; (2) you work in a large, highly visible company such as GM and the FTC chooses to monitor the company regularly with the objective of catching someone in the act of harassment, for the purpose of getting "press coverage" and warning as many potential harassers as possible.

Situation 2 is similar to the tendency of the IRS, right about tax time every year, to announce a story about a company that got caught violating some provision of the tax code that the IRS is clamping down on hard this year. The irony in the harassment statutes is that they cover primarily the collector and say very little about what the debtors have to do to play fair and be responsible about their debts. The problem with this "oversight" is that, to a collector, the debtors are harassing the collector much more than the collector is harassing the debtors.

Do you harass anybody? Probably not. Would you do it deliberately? Not likely. Are the laws reasonable? Sure, because some collectors need to be reined in, and the professional collectors don't need deception, threats, or that sort of thing to be a good collector.

I recall overhearing one day a top collection agency collector responding to a debtor who had accused her of harassing

him. Her response was factual and to the point, "Sir, you purchased a sofa on June 12 of this year in the amount of $395.
You have paid $100. Wilmont Furniture has tried for four
months to get you to pay the balance. After ignoring their
calls and notes, they assigned the account to us for collection.
I sent you a notice on this a week ago, and you did not call
back or pay. This phone call is about your account. Those are
the facts, sir. Do you have any questions?" The response from
a chastened debtor began with, "No, ma'am." I realize the
collector sounded like the old "Dragnet"—Just the facts,
ma'am—but it worked.

---

*Conclusion: Bluffing, lying, deception, threats,
and the like never worked long term anyway—now, thanks
to the FTC, they're also illegal.*

21

Skiptracing—How Sherlock Holmes Would Collect

_____

"Skiptracing"—the word evokes images of the pattern a flat stone flung across a lake makes. In the world of collecting, skiptracing is much less romantic, but it's essential in getting the total job done.

A skip is a debtor who doesn't want to be located or who has money he or she doesn't want you to know about. Of the $30 billion turned over to collection agencies each year, one-third, or $10 billion a year, is due to skips. The enormity of this number isn't surprising when you consider the mobility of people in the United States. Twenty percent of the population moves each year, either from where they live or work, and the moves directly affect consumer skips and consumer debt.

Skiptracing includes the decisions made and the actions taken to locate skips. You need to ask yourself two questions before you start to skiptrace:

1. Even if I find the debtor, can I collect?

2. Is it worth my time and money to skiptrace? Is the amount owed large enough?

Skips can be deliberate or unintentional. Knowing which is which helps in deciding how much effort to put into skiptracing. *Intentional* skips include:

- People with shallow or no roots. They change addresses often, live in hotels, mobile homes, trailer parks, low-income rental units or with friends and relatives. These people seldom acquire property, owe many people, and are used to being pursued by creditors. They may change jobs frequently, partly to avoid garnishment of their wages.
- Skips resulting from divorce, typically the former husband, who may skip across state lines.
- The credit criminal. You already know that he has no intention of paying, gives false information, and avoids all creditors.

Unintentional skips are more collectible. They're irresponsible in that they don't notify creditors of their move, and they don't arrange to have mail forwarded. They may be burdened with debt and decide to move to get a fresh start. If you find them, you may have a fairly good chance of collecting.

Skiptracing should be done as soon as the problem surfaces. However, it makes sense to back off if any of the following situations occur:

- Debtor's past payment record suggests a poor likelihood of payment even if the debtor is found.
- The amount due is too small to justify the time spent in skiptracing.
- Previous skiptracing work on this debtor yielded no results.
- Initial efforts indicate that the debtor is a credit criminal.

Begin skiptracing if (1) mail is returned; (2) the phone is

disconnected; (3) debtor changes address; (4) debtor's employment has terminated. Skiptrace for assets if the debtor (1) doesn't return phone calls; (2) promises to pay but doesn't; (3) offers a small payment, even though your credit information suggests that he can pay more, and he refuses to update the credit information or substantiate his low payment offer; (4) refuses to pay.

Before you begin a skiptrace, you also need a policy that takes into account the relative value of account balances. For example,

1. Skiptrace only balances over $100.
2. Write off and immediately assign for collection all skips under $100.
3. On balances from $100 to $1000, contact only the leads on the customer credit information form. If you get no results, assign the accounts for collection.
4. For balances over $1000, check library resources, tax assessor's records, credit bureau information, and the Department of Motor Vehicles.

As you can see, skiptracing can be a tedious, time-consuming, detail-oriented bit of business. Still, done properly, it can make you money or, more accurately, reduce your losses in a cost-justified manner. Besides, no book on collecting would be complete without a strong handle on skiptracing.

Locating Skips

We look next at the sources of skiptracing information. I'll discuss how to use some of the more powerful ones. Here are the main places/people to check for locating skips:

1. *Customer credit information form* is your best starting point.

2. *Mail return* is often the first sign of a skip. Leads here may quickly locate the debtor.

3. *Telephone directory* is often overlooked. The debtor may have a new listed address and phone number.

4. *Similar last names.* Calls to the same or similar last names often produce leads.

5. *City and suburban directories* are arranged alphabetically by name, numerically by street address, or numerically by phone number.

6. *Cross street directories* are arranged by address and list published phone subscribers and their phone numbers at the address.

7. *Relatives, neighbors, friends* provide clues about where debtors have gone, who else may know them, where they work.

8. *Neighborhood stores* provide good leads if the debtor has lived in the area for some time.

9. *Former employers.* The Personnel Departments may not help, but fellow employees often will know where the debtor now works and will feel free to give out the information.

10. *Landlords, janitors, superintendents* are talkative sources of information.

11. *Voter registration records* contain not only home address but type of employment.

12. *Assessor's Office.* Public records reveal if your debtor owns real estate. If the debtor is a skip, the building owner may have information about where she moved.

13. *Death and probate records* establish who claimed the body and whether or not an estate is being probated.

14. *Divorce records* establish date of divorce and address of a former spouse.

15. *Motor Vehicle records* are prime tools for establishing new addresses, either through vehicle or driver's license information.

16. *Bankruptcy filing.* If your account is included, forget skiptracing work (see Chapter 19).

17. *Credit bureau records* provide loads of information about debtor's paying habits plus many leads for skiptracing.

18. *Referring business* may have information you don't have.

19. *Religious or other group affiliations, employment affiliations, other creditors,* such as banks, stores, finance companies.

Credit Information Form

Most of the skiptracing you'll do to locate a debtor will consist of calling leads from this form. As you gather the information, decide whether to continue skiptracing, write the account off, or assign it for collection. Be sure to ask for:

1. Customer name: full first, middle, and last name.

2. Guarantor name, if other than customer: full first, middle and last name. Full names ensure that you have the right person when you're dealing with a common name. Even uncommon names are often duplicated in directories or public records.

3. Current home address and phone number.

4. *Complete* employment information on all guarantors (usually husband and wife for consumer debt), including job title, length of time employed, and a direct phone number to the guarantor at the guarantor's job location.

5. Relatives or personal friends.

6. Who, if anyone, referred the customer.

7. Social security number and date of birth—used when securing credit bureau or driver's license information, distinguishing between debtors, or sorting out who's responsible.

8. Bank account. If the customer doesn't give you this

information, record it from a check written by the customer. Get the bank, branch, and account number.

9. Credit references, which give you information to skiptrace, can tell you whether or not you should skiptrace further, and can yield asset information that will justify a lawsuit.

Mail Returns—Different Types

The post office normally indicates the type of mail return, which gives you clues about what kind of skip you have and what to do about it.

Mail Return—No Such Street

You may have used the wrong street or even the wrong city. Check your records. A new customer may give you a wrong or incomplete street or city, which is a good reason for asking for identification. What to do?

1. See if you transferred information correctly from the credit form to the billing records.
2. Call the debtor. If unsuccessful, check the crisscross directory for same-named streets in nearby communities.
3. Call the post office, give them the zip code, and ask what city the zip code corresponds to.

Mail Return—No Such Number

See if any parts of the street number are transposed. Check your records. Call the customer if you find no error. Check information and phone directories if you can't reach the customer.

Mail Return—Address Unknown

This is a real skip. Start calling the leads, beginning with the home phone number on the credit information form.

Mail Return—Moved, Left No Address

This is also a real skip.

Look for handwritten messages on returned envelopes, such as "He died" or "Deceased" or "I moved." These notations are likely to be written by a debtor who's still living at the address you mailed to.

You can reduce mail skips if you have all your billings stamped or preprinted Address Correction Requested on the face of the envelope, upper left-hand corner. If your customer has requested that the post office forward his mail, you'll get your envelope back with the new address. If you want the envelope to be sent on to a new address, add the words Forwarding Postage Guaranteed to the envelope. The post office discontinues this service after six to twelve months.

Library Information

Your local public library has resources that let you do heavy-duty skiptracing. Three sources in particular are worthwhile:

Phone Directories for Other Cities

Check the alphabetic section for last names similar to that of your debtor. Check the yellow pages for businesses similar to ones your debtor worked at or owned.

City and Suburban Directories

Information on businesses and households, obtained by canvassing, appears in various directories. R. L. Polk & Company, the major printer of these directories, issues periodic updates for major metropolitan areas, consisting of the following sections:

1. Alphabetic list of area residences and businesses. Information can include lead name, spouse, marital status, occupation, residence address, home phone, and whether or not home is owned. Similar information can be gathered for local businesses.
2. Street address section arranged alphabetically by street and then by number. This section lists householder name and phone number.
3. Numerical phone section. This section lists numerically phone numbers and the name of the person to whom the phone is listed.

Cross Phone Directories

Usually called crisscross or reverse directories, these are published by the phone company and may be updated every three to six months. These directories contain listings of streets and, by house number for each street, the listed subscriber and phone number.

Credit Bureau Information

To get information from a credit bureau, you must be a member or arrange access through a member. The information can help you in four ways. First, credit bureau data can reveal sources of the debtor's and spouse's income or other assets needed to justify filing a lawsuit. Second, the data may reflect the debtor's payment history with creditors and will show any liens or judgment against him. Third, the information will expand considerably your ability to skiptrace by providing the names of other creditors to contact. Finally, information will enable you to decide more accurately your debtor's borrowing power.

Assessor Records

The tax assessor maintains records on all property in the county, showing who owns the parcel, the mailing address for the tax statement, and the assessed value of the land and improvements. These records can be checked alphabetically by name to find out if a debtor owns multiple properties or to establish who owns a parcel at a particular address. This information has several uses:

1. Property ownership is a major asset that can help justify filing a lawsuit.
2. If a debtor owns property, she can usually use it as collateral to borrow money.
3. You can call the owner of an apartment building where your debtor lives and ask the owner where the debtor works and banks. If the debtor has moved, the owner may know the new address or provide other leads.

Getting Information From Sources

Once you've developed sources of information for skiptracing debtors, you need a strategy for getting information from those sources. Some sources may have been stung by your debtor and will be only too helpful in telling you anything you want to know, to "get even" with your common enemy. Other sources may be the debtor's friends or relatives and have no interest whatever in helping you. They may consider all businesses their common enemy and will alert your debtor, warning her to go even deeper into hiding.

To complicate the job of skiptracing further, you can't use deception, nor can you give derogatory information to people who don't need to know it. A good example of deception concerns a crack skiptracer in Seattle. She used to call a debtor's relative, and say that she had a box of pineapples for the debtor, just off the boat from Hawaii, the pineapples were starting to go bad, and she just *had* to get hold of the debtor-relative. The ploy worked for a long time, but now it's in clear violation of debt collection statutes. An example of improperly giving information is to say to a debtor's neighbor that you're looking for the debtor because she owes you money.

Here are strategies and tactics for getting information. You must create a sense of urgency, but don't give the informant the third degree. The following sequence works well:

1. Be sure you have the correct informant. Ask, "Is this Mrs. Wilma Foster at 123 Broadway?"
2. Identify yourself. "Mrs. Foster, this is Joan Wilson."
3. State the problem. "I need to get in touch with David Peterson."
4. Ask for help: "Can you help me?"
5. Listen carefully. Your informant will usually state or signal whether or not he knows your debtor and where he can be reached. He may also let you know if this is a good time to ask questions.
6. Ask key questions:
   a. "Do you know where he is?"
   b. "Where did he work?"
   c. "Where does Sarah, his wife, work?"
   d. "Do you know anyone else who might know where to reach him?"
7. You can ask "wrong" questions; people love to correct you. So, for example, if you don't know where David

works, you can ask, "Does David still work at the post office?"

When you call for information, resistance is inevitable. Here are the four key questions to expect and how to finesse them. In each case, you answer the question put to you and then you follow immediately with a question of your own.

1. *"Who did you say this is?"* You: "This is Joan Wilson. Where can I get in touch with David? I really need to talk to him."
2. *"What do you want him for?"* You: "Something important has come up I have to talk to him about. Do you know anyone who can help me?" Or, "It's a business matter that's important to both David and me, and I've lost touch. Do you have a number where I can reach him?"
3. *"Does he owe you money?"* You: "Unfortunately, it's a personal matter he wouldn't want me to discuss. Do you know where he's working?"
4. *"Are you a bill collector?"* You: "Unfortunately, state and federal laws don't allow me to reveal exactly why I'm trying to reach David. It's confidential business."

Skiptracing, like collecting, contains a high degree of selling technique. You have to qualify the prospect and deal with resistance. It's also plain hard work. Therefore, it makes sense to minimize the need for doing it. The best single tool available to you for preventing skips and assisting in skiptracing is the original credit application form.

Assets

Assets have unequal value and justify unequal amounts of time to locate. In a number of states, such as Texas and North Carolina, even if you find some excellent assets, they do you little or no good in collecting. In most other states, assets can be converted into money for you according to the following scale, starting with the most liquid at the beginning. In every case, you need a judgment from a court first. There are no longer any prejudgment attachments unless you represent the IRS or proceed under RICO statutes on racketeering.

Bank Account (Checking and Savings)

This is the most liquid asset. If the money is in the account, you can get it all, up to the amount of your judgment.

Employee Salary

The salary is the second easiest source of money, if you have a judgment. Most states allow wage garnishment, although federal law limits the amount to 25 percent of disposable income, with a base amount exempted. You may have to do several garnishments to satisfy the judgment in full.

Real Estate

Real estate isn't liquid at all, but if you file a lien on the debtor's real estate, your bill will have to be paid if the debtor wants to sell or refinance the property.

Other Assets

Included in these assets are motor vehicles, furniture, jewelry, livestock, rental income, and business equipment. Note that they're difficult to execute on.

Cash Business Owned by a Debtor

As mentioned in Chapter 14, in most states you can send in a sheriff or a marshall, with a judgment, to the business to remove the money in the cash drawer, either all at once or as it comes in. These procedures are commonly called a keeper or a till-tap.

New phone company technology is making some of the grunt work of skiptracing easier and more cost efficient. Your business can now obtain direct access to phone company directory information so that you don't have to go through an information operator and be limited to three numbers per inquiry. These systems allow you to verify addresses and phone numbers at the rate of several hundred an hour and at a cost lower than that for manual inquiry. By 1990, your business will have direct access to the phone company's reverse directory. This technology is a boon for skiptracing and address verification.

Conclusion: Skiptracing is a pain. Prevent it when you can, do it quickly when you must, and don't hesitate to quickly use a third-party professional when the trail gets cold.

22

Especially for Healthcare— The Industry with Unhealthy Collections

W arning! Don't be surprised if you get some nifty ideas from this chapter, even if your business is neither doctor nor hospital. The healthcare people have so many self-inflicted collection wounds, and many of their business practices are carried out by other types of businesses in similar ways. As you read about these healthcare business problems, you might notice an occasional sign of recognition. (In the following chapter, I examine several other businesses whose traditional collection strategies can teach you lessons about how to improve or carry out more skillfully the strategies presented here.)

I admit a special attraction to the collection problems of doctors and hospitals. Healthcare practitioners, as they're called collectively, are considered among the worst business-people. They need help!

Doctors in training learn almost nothing about the business aspect of their practices. Business concepts are foreign, and doctors are the first choice of investment promoters pitching sales of practically anything. If you can step into the shoes of a healthcare business, you can get a broad understanding of how a business can shoot itself in the foot—reduce its rate of growth and minimize its earnings.

As for brains, supposedly no one is smarter than a doctor. We'll see how this overwhelming firepower in the left brain leaves the best-intentioned doctor helpless in the face of even the most inexperienced patient who doesn't feel like paying. But hospitals are much better, you say? They have professionals managing the business functions, don't they? And, if they falter, aren't there always large, sophisticated chains like Humana available to run them properly? We'll see.

Let's look at the healthcare business as it really is. This is a long chapter, so I'll cut down on the philosophizing in the interest of brevity.

Hospitals' Collection Problems

Runaway Costs

Because people are living longer, the cost of prolonging life grows exponentially as a person's age advances, insurance premiums are increasing at a speed close to the inflation rate during the Weimar Republic, hospitals—particularly in rural areas—are going out of business, closing wings, and merging.

Poorly Run Business Offices

Hospital business offices are usually understaffed; money is spent on a $700,000 CAT scanner instead of a collector. Financial policies, if they exist, are kept secret from patients and often from business office personnel as well. Hospitals hold on to unpaid accounts almost as long as do the doctors, who hold on to their unpaid accounts twice as long as they should.

Too Many Unexpected Bills

Patients in a hospital can receive as many as seven different bills. One bill is from the hospital on discharge; another one is received from the hospital because all the bills weren't submitted to the cashier when the patient left the hospital. A third bill may be from the anesthesiologist, the fourth one from pathology (testing lab). Bill five to seven may be from radiology (X rays) and an assistant surgeon or two. *And nobody from the hospital told the patient that seven different bills would be sent*! How do you think patients react when they get the third, fourth, etc. bill?

Weak Payment Policies

Hospital administrators are very public relations conscious. They want the money, but they don't want to appear hard-nosed, which would encourage doctors to admit patients elsewhere. As a result, payment policies are usually wishy-washy.

Admitting Doctors

Doctors with admitting privileges at hospitals add to the burden. When they admit a patient, they seldom tell the patient anything about the hospital payment policy or the fact that the patient could get multiple bills.

None of this is done out of ill-will, selfishness, or other less-than-noble motives. I think that healthcare providers contribute to their own collection problems for four primary reasons.

1. *Naiveté*. Providers assume that patients are experts in healthcare reimbursement. In fact, patients seldom know what their present insurance coverage is, and they often receive a new plan every year.
2. *Unwillingness to discuss money too forthrightly.* Healthcare providers don't want to appear money hungry.
3. *Attitude of doctors.* Doctors have a slight tendency to expect a superior standard of living and a preference for staying above the fray on business matters. The staff is left to wallow, unguided, in the complex world of fees and payments.
4. *Fear of loss.* Providers fear that if they press too hard for payment, patients will take their business elsewhere.

Solving the Problems

Eight specific steps will help hospitals solve their collection problems. Paradoxically, the solutions will also increase their business.

1. Establish and maintain a clear, written financial policy. Make the policy available to all patients prior to their admission. Spell out *exactly* how hospital's charges are generated and paid.
2. Financial counselors should examine all inpatient admissions or high-dollar outpatient services such as same-day surgery or radiation therapy. If a patient is a self-pay or the insurance is less than 80 percent, attempt to collect self-pay balances, deductibles, and copayments.
3. Procedures should include identifying previously incurred bad debt and provide the ability to deny service in elective, nonemergency cases where there's doubt of payment.
4. In the emergency room, ask guarantors and all con-

scious patients for identification. Ask for minimum payment. Get a credit card number to charge for treatment.

5. Train staff offices—those with admitting privileges—to explain hospital financial policy and why it will benefit those admitting doctors' offices and their patients to know about the policy.

6. Train business office people. Send them to seminars on collections. Conduct regular staff meetings. Review policy and how it's implemented. Conduct role-playing exercises on collections.

7. Set goals on Patient Days Outstanding. This measure of accounts receivable control is familiar to all hospitals.

8. For receivables temporarily out of control, hire collection temporaries who'll return $4 to $5 for each $1 spent on them. Use the money in the training budget or the general fund, even though you can't get enough FTEs (full-time equivalents).

The appendix illustrates a sample financial policy for a hospital.

Doctors' Collection Problems

Doctors have complex collection problems. Doctors feel as if they're victims of the system: If their problems aren't exacerbated by ungrateful patients who put doctor bills at the bottom of the list, then the insurance companies are surely to blame for their cash flow agonies. Of course, this is nonsense.

The collection problems of doctors, like those of any credit grantor, are caused by the doctor 100 percent.

If that sounds harsh, consider the corollary. Because the doctor causes the collection problems, only he or she can clear them up. What a wonderful prescription; the solution to the problem is in one's own hands. You don't have to seek the kindness of strangers for the way out of the morass.

What I'm haranguing about is a point of view, one that I think is accurate. Doctors can't expect insurance companies to transform themselves and suddenly start paying all claims instantly. If anything, the companies have an incentive to hang onto the payment money as long as possible, to earn money (interest) on their money.

Slow-Paying Patients

Expecting patients to pay quicker is another leap into fantasy. Every doctor's office does have a policy, but it's usually the patient's policy. The policy of most patients is something like this: I'll pay you when I'm good and ready, in an amount that doesn't inconvenience me too much. And if I have insurance, let's you and me wait and see what the insurance company pays until I pay you anything. That thought process chills the marrow of every doctor's assistant, but it shows clearly that changes in collection results can come only from the doctor's office, not from the payment sources.

The way to proceed is to develop a clear financial policy, put it in writing, give a copy of it to each patient, and discuss it with patients when they call in, come in, and after treatment. You'll acknowledge that your policy may be different from that of other doctors but you have this policy because your business manager has advised you that it works best for most patients. Ask for feedback on your policy. If none is forthcoming, direct the patient's attention to those areas that confuse most patients or that most patients resist. Such areas include how *you* get paid when the patient has insurance.

You'll get resistance from many patients, particularly established ones who paid under a previously easy policy. You won't justify your new policy by whining about how your costs are going up. Your patients could care less, that's not their problem, and they think you make too much money anyway. Don't expect sympathy. Just tell them your policy. If pushed, explain that the business manager recommended it and that's that.

Phone Quotes

Patients may call in on the phone asking for your fees. But how can you quote a fee if you haven't seen the patient? Even if the patient says she wants only a physical exam, or a teeth cleaning and X rays, you don't know what your diagnosis will be, what treatment will be needed, and what the cost of that unknown treatment will be. But if you refuse to quote any cost at all, you lose the patient. Some people are phone shoppers, and they can be induced to buy (yes, patients are consumers). With a patient you've never seen before, you'll probably want to be paid in full at the time of the visit, but if you won't tell the patient a fee, how can she know how much money to bring?

The solution is simple: Quote a range based on your experience, and the odds. Here's a dialogue for a new patient who calls up and wants to know what it will cost if he comes in to have a boil lanced:

> You: That depends, of course, on where the boil is, how big it is, and other factors, so we won't know exactly until the doctor examines you. But in our experience, the fee ranges from $50 on the low side to $125 for a complex case, so if you'll bring in $125, that will cover it nine times out of ten.

That's full disclosure. If the patient goes elsewhere, don't you think you might be better off since the patient didn't respond positively to your honesty?

Dismissing a Patient

Taking on new patients, as we've just examined, has inherent collection risks. And ending the relationship involves peculiar problems too. All doctors have patients they'd like to "fire," usually because the patients don't pay in an acceptable manner. When firing a patient, you must avoid charges of abandonment. If you do decide that you've had enough aggravation from a slow or nonpaying patient, send the following letter by certified mail, return receipt requested, with a copy filed in the patient's records.

Dear_____:

I find it necessary to inform you that I am withdrawing further professional attendance upon you.

I suggest that you place yourself under the care of another physician without delay.

If you so desire, I shall be available to attend you for a reasonable time after you have received this letter, but in no event for more than thirty days.

This should give you ample time to select a physician of your choice from the many competent practitioners in this city. With your approval, I will make available to this physician your case history and information regarding the diagnosis and treatment that you have received from me.

You may obtain information as to other treating physicians by contacting the _____ Medical Society at

_____.

Very truly yours,

When terminating services, the key elements in any letter you send are

1. Certified mail, return receipt requested.
2. Allow thirty days for the patient to find another doctor.
3. Give a referral source the patient can use to find another doctor. Don't give a list of names yourself.
4. Treat emergencies in the intervening thirty days.

To repeat for the umpteenth time, check all legal-sounding advice with your attorney. Not only am I not an attorney, even if I were, I'm not your attorney. Be careful.

Another question that arises when you fire a patient and you haven't been paid concerns the diagnostic records. You should forward the records immediately. If you don't, you may be contributing to an incomplete or improper diagnosis, which leaves you open to a malpractice suit.

Speaking of malpractice, some debtors, when pressed to pay, threaten malpractice, which usually makes the collector back off fast. How seriously should you take such a threat? *Very* seriously.

Experience shows that most malpractice threats never get carried out; they're used to avoid payment. However, it doesn't hurt to follow these prudent steps. Ask the patient what, specifically, the complaint is about. Say that you'll check into it, but try again for payment. Check with the malpractice carrier.

In some states, you can be fully protected from phony malpractice claims through a procedure involving what's known as the date of discovery. For example, suppose there's a one-year date of discovery on a claim. You discussed payment with the patient within that year and nothing was mentioned about malpractice. If you wait a year from the time of treatment and then press hard for payment, and the patient then screams malpractice, she or he won't get away with it in court.

No Shows

Some doctors are so busy that a broken appointment or two is a relief. But for many practices, a no-show is a loss of income, is an inconvenience, denies you the opportunity to contact another patient for treatment, and affects your attitude. Doctors like to charge for no-shows, but they fear such patient reactions as, "You want to charge me for wasting your time? Let's discuss all the times I sat in your waiting room for forty-five minutes with magazines no more recent than 1986!" It does make you pause.

My solution is a clear, unambiguous external policy backed up by a flexible internal policy. The external policy says, "Unless we have twenty-four hour's notice of your inability to keep your appointment, there will be a $15 charge." That's straightforward; patients know exactly what to expect. Just having a policy like that in writing, fully communicated to all patients, will automatically reduce the incidence of no-shows because now there are consequences for not showing up. The way to alter human behavior is with consequences. If little Johnny throws a rock through a window, do you give him an ice cream cone for doing that? No—you probably paddle his little bottom and send him to bed. Johnny will be less likely to repeat the incident (unless he's starved for attention, but that's another matter).

You add to the effectiveness of your no-show policy by how you enforce it with your internal policy. For example, if the no-show was as the result of an emergency, I wouldn't charge for that. I wouldn't put that fact in writing either, because if I did, every no-show would invent an emergency. People aren't stupid.

If there isn't an emergency and you receive no notice or less than twenty-four hour's notice, your three basic options are:

1. Telling the patient, for a first-time no-show, "This is the first time this has happened, so we don't want to charge you for it this time." You're implying that the patient shouldn't do it again and you aren't setting a precedent.
2. Telling the patient you'll see if you can get the fee cut a bit, leave for thirty seconds, and then return telling patient you got it cut to $5. You may get some appreciation for bending the rules.
3. Charging the full fee for a chronic appointment breaker. Eventually, you may have to fire the patient.

Patients with Insurance

A main area of aggravation for doctors is getting paid when patients have insurance. Patients tend to think that their insurance will pay 110 percent, at least. Patients don't want to hear that they're fully responsible for bills even though they're insured; you need to go out of your way to educate patients about this point.

If the insurance company is slow in paying, patients expect the doctor to check out the delay. Unfortunately, insurance companies have no incentive to respond to inquiries by the providers (doctors and hospitals) because providers don't pay insurance premiums; the patients or employers do. What we have is a massive amount of misunderstanding to correct. Who has to correct it? Right—the doctor or the hospital are the only ones.

Before diving into this complex subject, I want to digress into a lighter aspect of it. It's tough enough getting paid by insurance companies when you do everything right. But some practices unnecessarily add to their problems. To explain, let me discuss Norman Johnson, senior claims examiner for Tolley International Corporation, which administers more than 1000 employee benefit plans.

In the course of processing insurance claims, Johnson has encountered all sorts of mysterious maladies. These less-than-literate doctor's diagnoses are guaranteed to slow up payment. How fast can you expect to be paid for "impounded teeth," "erotic bowels," "cologne trouble," or "gastric dizzy stress"? What insurance codes would you use for "Aunt Jemimah pectoris," "gald blatter atak," or "Hi Per Tension"?

Serious payment delays can be expected for "blabbar-trouble," "Protestant trouble," and "authoritis." As for "science trouble," "kid knees operation," or "information of the eyeball," forget it. And, if you really want to impoverish your patient, try a "removal of the prosperous glands." Enough. On to serious business with insurance. I want to discuss three key issues that cause collection problems whenever patients have insurance.

Policy

What should your policy be for patients with insurance? You have three basic options (starting with the worst). With option 1, you wait to see what the insurance company pays before making the patient pay anything. This is the favorite of most patients. It's used commonly by doctors who fear offending patients, but it does neither patient nor doctor any good.

The policy is bad for the doctor because it unnecessarily delays payment. It's bad for the patient because it supports a fantasy that the patient isn't responsible for the bill, and I don't believe in reinforcing this type of fantasy. Some fantasies, such as soap operas, are fine, but not a payment fantasy.

Option 2, a better policy, derives from the fact that insurance, after deductibles are paid, typically pays 80 percent of many bills. Therefore, you can ask for at least 20 percent of the estimated fee at the time of treatment. However, the reality is that 20 percent may not be enough. I prefer that you ask for 25 percent to 30 percent. Then, when the insurance money comes in, you can either refund the credit balance immediately or leave it on the account.

Leaving the credit balance on account is not that farfetched. Increasingly, doctors who see patients on a regular basis, such as allergists or chiropractors, ask for a chunk of money paid up front; the doctor then works off the balance until the money needs to be replenished.

If you don't ask, you don't get. If you do ask and encounter resistance to paying in advance, you can always back down to payment at the time of treatment. You'll still avoid billing.

Option 3 is far and away the best policy. Because you treat patients, not insurance companies, you're well within your rights and sound business procedure to ask patients to pay the entire amount of the bill on the day of treatment. Then help the patients with their insurance forms so that they'll be reimbursed directly by their insurance company. Few practices have the courage to put this policy into effect. Those that do report that they hardly lose any patients, and the policy certainly has done wonders for reducing collection aggravations.

I'd like to reiterate at this point that I never tell any credit grantor what their financial policy should be. After all, who am I to tell you to whom you should give away your services or products? That's a personal, subjective matter. What I have much to say about is your need to decide what your policy is and how to communicate it so that all customers (patients) know what to expect, up front, prior to doing business, as much as possible.

Assignment of Benefits

The Assignment of Benefits is a document the patient signs that authorizes the insurance company to pay provider directly instead of sending the payment to the patient. The problem is that insurance companies commonly send payment to the patient anyway, even though there's a valid assignment. Some patients who receive this money deny that they got it; others admit that they received it but had better things to do with the money than pay you.

To compound your misery, the insurance companies tell you that this is your problem—you'll have to get the money from the patient. We're talking serious stress here. To begin sorting out this mess, if you've confirmed that the patient received the money and refuses to pay, you can sue or turn him into collection. His denials are no defense.

As for the insurance company, tell them that sending the check to the patient is their problem. They will have to ask for it back and, in the meantime, they need to send a check to you, now. And they do need to do that. The insurance company will probably deny any responsibility. To wake them up, point out that you will ask the patient to contact the insurance commissioner to have that office check into this matter.

The Insurance Commission—every state has one— regulates insurance companies who do business in your state, regardless of where the companies are headquartered. The commissioner serves consumers, your patients, and is likely to be on your side when an insurance company transgresses. Call your state's insurance commissioner and get a copy of the statutes that regulate insurance matters, such as how long an insurance company can dispute a bill, how quickly they have to pay, etc.

Delaying Tactics

You send in a perfectly filled out insurance claim—all the I's are dotted, the T's crossed, and all accompanying documents attached. A problem arises when the insurance company asks for another copy of the claim or a repeat of the information you've already sent. This is a classic delaying tactic. The best way I've heard of reducing this type of insurance game playing is to send a letter on your letterhead that states essentially the following:

> Before we send you the information you are requesting, which, by the way, we already sent you on July 12, we will require our administrative fee of $45 by return mail.

Three things usually happen:

1. The company will pay your ridiculous administrative fee.
2. The company will pay your claim faster.
3. The company will hassle someone else.

The amount of $45 isn't high; I know of offices that charge more than $100. This ploy works for two reasons. First, every insurance company has a budget for such expenses. Second, the money isn't coming out of the pockets of the clerks who handle the claims, so they don't care. This little secret is like one learned by experienced airline travellers.

These pros know you don't have to eat standard airline food, commonly known as mystery meals. There are available dozens of special meals, such as vegetarian, seafood, lowfat, high protein, etc., etc. These meals tend to be fresher, in larger quantity, and don't cost you a penny more. I always order either seafood or vegetarian and get, in addition to a better meal, envious stares by my neighbors. The airlines don't publicize this little secret any more than do insurance companies who will pay you for the trouble of getting information for them.

Another little used but very effective technique with slow-moving insurance companies is to send them to collection, particularly with an inexpensive precollection letter service. This communication goes to a supervisor, not a clerk, and definitely gets the claim off the bottom of the stack.

Discussing Money After Treatment

I've discussed presenting your financial policy up front prior to treatment every chance you get. But suppose you can't discuss fees in advance. Suppose, for example, a patient is wheeled in comatose (unconscious). Or suppose a patient is zonked out of his mind on drugs and has no idea that a doctor is in attendance. Obviously, you're going to have to discuss money after treatment, as soon as possible.

I'd like to show you how to handle one of the most difficult examples of discussing money after treatment. It concerns a consulting psychiatrist who's invited to come to a hospital to treat a patient admitted there.

Predictable patient reactions, when asked to pay, are likely to include: I didn't ask you to treat me, and I'm not cured, so why should I pay? The best solution is to call the patient immediately upon discharge and say the following:

> Patient, Williams Memorial Hospital called Dr. Arnold in to treat you, as is their legal right to do. Dr. Arnold is certified in psychiatry, is fully qualified to treat you, and did so to the best of his skill and ability.
>
> The bill that you are about to receive from our office is for that treatment, will be in addition to any other bill you get from the hospital or other doctors or labs, and needs to be handled directly with us. Do you have any questions about that?

Let me highlight why this approach is so effective:

1. You communicated verbally and immediately instead of hoping a written message on a bill would make the points you need to get across.
2. You acknowledged the probable resistance points (the patient not asking for your doctor to come in and not feeling cured).
3. You acknowledged that there will be other bills, some of which will be paid differently than yours.
4. You gave the patient a chance to respond, which lets you know right away if you were dealing with an above-the-line or below-the-line debtor.
5. You followed up in writing what you said on the phone.

Notice that so many of the areas of resistance are predictable. Because they are, it's easy to knock them down by acknowledging them and answering your own points.

Radiology, pathology, and anesthesiology are three other specialties in which this technique pays off. Here are the predictable resistances to payment that you have to acknowledge:

1. *Radiology* (X rays). "I don't understand why my regular doctor didn't read those pictures. How do I know I needed them at all, and isn't the charge kind of high?"
2. *Pathology* (tests on tissues and fluids). "I didn't authorize those tests. I'm sure you did more than you needed, and why didn't you include this bill with the other bills?"
3. *Anesthesiology.* "I already got a bill for anesthesia from the hospital, and I never saw your doctor."

These solutions will solve the problem.

Radiology

Somebody should tell the patient in advance that a separate charge for X rays is normal. In addition, the radiologist's first bill should include a separate sheet of paper, preferably in a color different from the bill, headed by the words URGENT—PLEASE READ THIS FIRST and then stating, in large type,

> We took and interpreted X-rays upon the recommendation of your doctor, for the purpose of helping ensure your well-being.
> Your doctor has the legal right to order these X rays, and we reported the results to your doctor.
> The bill enclosed with this notice is for our services and is entirely separate from any other bills you may receive as a result of your treatment.
> Payment to us in the full amount shown on your bill is expected at this time.
> Thank you.

Pathology

The same type of note as the radiologists use is used here also. In addition, because the pathology lab seldom sees patients and the volume of billing can be very high, billing every ten days to two weeks is much more effective than billing once a month.

Anesthesiology

In addition to sending a bill, personnel need to call right after the operation and explain that the anesthesia charge on the hospital bill is for the hospital's anesthesia products, delivery, and monitoring systems. The anesthesiologist's bill is for the physician who administered the anesthesia. Patients are constantly surprised—unnecessarily—by anesthesia bills. Here's a personal example of how easy it is to avoid misunderstandings and let the patient know, in advance, about the person who administers the anesthesia.

A few years ago, I needed arthroscopic surgery on my left knee. The night before the operation, while I was watching television, I got a phone call from a man asking for me.

After I identified myself, he said, "I understand you're having an operation on your knee at Peninsula Hospital tomorrow." I replied, "Yes. How did you know?" He answered, "Well, my name is Dr. Robert Brown, and I'm the anesthesiologist for your operation. When I see you tomorrow morning, I'm going to hook you up to a life support system. I'm the guy that's going to keep you alive!"

Well, I assure you that he got my full attention. I got up, shut off the television set, and asked him to tell me more. It became quite obvious that there was a separate provider in the picture. He never mentioned money. He didn't have to.

Specialists

Specialists of all stripes have a major collection strike against them, or so it seems. A specialist is a provider who gets patients from another doctor, usually the general practitioner. Because the specialist sees the patient only once or a few times and never again, payment policies have to be more direct than those of the primary care doctor, who has many opportunities to handle payment.

The problem is that if the specialist is vague about money, he'll have many referrals, but will also experience an unacceptable level of uncollectible accounts.

On the other hand, a payment policy that's too tough will yield few collection problems, but there's a danger of choking off the flow of referrals because patients will complain to the referring doctor.

The solution is inherent in the problem. The specialist needs two avenues of communication: One with patients (as all credit grantors need to do) and one, the more difficult avenue, with the many doctors who refer patients to the specialist. Because everyone's main objective is to serve the patient's need to know about fees and services, the specialist must have a series of conversations with each referring doctor. The conversations can be conducted staff member to staff member or doctor to doctor.

Here's a sample dialogue from a doctor who's a specialist to a doctor who sends him patients:

> "You know, Dave, when your office sends me patients, some of them aren't 100 percent sure they need my services, and some of the others assume my bill is included in your fee."
>
> What would work really well for your patients is this, I think. When your assistant sends a patient to me, have her tell the patient that you're sending them to me for their best health interests since I'm a specialist with special training, and you don't want to take chances. Add that I handle fees separate from the way your office does it.
>
> Then, when your patient comes down to my office, my assistant will confirm what your assistant said, and your patient will know exactly where he stands on fees and services and he'll really appreciate that, don't you think?

And that does make a lot of sense.

Some people say they don't have enough time to "train" all the referring doctors that need to be contacted. To me, that's similar to a general practitioner saying she doesn't have enough time to discuss financial policy with patients. If you don't take the time prior to treatment, you'll spend the time *after* treatment, and you'll spend more time, I promise you. Also, the stress level after treatment will be much higher.

Workers Compensation

Workers Compensation claims are for work-related injuries. Payment may be a little slow, but the money does usually come in. Delay can occur when the circumstances of the injury require investigation. Follow up with the employer. If the employer gives you a case number, you have a claim. You may have to follow up with the carrier also. Even though the claim may be payable by an insurance carrier, most states allow you to request payment from the patient.

A bigger problem occurs if the case is eventually deemed not a Workers Compensation case. Then you have to seek payment from the patient, who doesn't want to hear about it. The solution, for all Workers Compensation cases, is to have the patient sign a document that confirms her awareness of an obligation to pay in full in the event that the carrier denies the claim. If a patient comes in for treatment for an injury resulting from an accident and claims that someone else is at fault and will pay, I suggest you avoid the temptation to wait and see how the case turns out—it may not come to trial for three years.

Legal Matters

As I recommended earlier, rather than accepting a lien or an attorney protection letter, get payment in full now or work out whatever payment arrangements you're willing to accept. If the patient and/or her attorney aren't cooperative, remind them that you're entirely within your rights to sue the patient right now if satisfactory arrangements aren't made.

Regarding another legal matter, doctors are sometimes asked to testify in court as expert witnesses and give depositions, which will be paid right after the court appearance. My response is this: Never go to court to give a deposition unless you're paid in advance. When you insist on that condition, you usually get it.

As you can see, doctors have to negotiate many landmines, mostly of their own doing. They learn nothing about collection problems in school. Typically, a doctor graduates, hangs out a shingle, and watches every deadbeat in town beat a path to her door. Eventually, she gets tired of this and puts a good, clear payment policy into effect or joins a group practice, hoping that the business manager will take care of collections.

Group Practices

Even group practices have inherent problems. Occasionally, a group allows itself one overall payment policy. But with a group of strong individuals, more likely each doctor will insist on his own policy, thus encouraging confusion among patients. When patients go to Doctor X, it's one policy. At Doctor Y, it's another. The patients ask, "How come?" The staff can only reply, "Well, Doctor X feels this way about fees and Doctor Y feels another way, which isn't surprising, since you probably feel still a third way yourself about them. It's true that they have different policies, and I want to be sure you know about that in advance." At least each doctor can be consistent within his office for the payment policy.

Other Obstructions

This chapter has been long because doctors are a microcosm of all credit grantors that provide services in ways that can be confusing and resented and that will meet with a predictable level of resistance. Each type of provider has its own special war stories. Ambulance companies are constantly picking people up off the pavement after an accident, taking them to the hospital, and then, when a bill is presented, having to listen to, "I didn't ask you to pick me up. Go bill the hospital." As a result, most ambulance companies bill twice a month.

Veterinarians have become very insistent on payment at the time their client brings an animal for treatment. Still, I hear stories from large-animal vets who go to a ranch to treat a horse, and the owner asks the vet to check out the rest of the stable. When the bill comes, the owner denies asking the vet for such service.

Dentists who use a lab for dentures or any appliance for the mouth are likely to insist on at least the lab fee before the patient leaves the office. If the dentist does crown and bridge work, the insurance coverage is closer to 50 percent, not 80 percent, so the patient must be sold a much higher patient payment.

What about big bills, such as those incurred when a child has orthodontic treatment? We're talking about several thousands of dollars, usually handled over many months. One problem facing the orthodontist is the guarantor who isn't paying as agreed. The doctor doesn't want to harm the patient by stopping treatment; fortunately, the doctor has considerable time before it's necessary to tighten the bands. Given the high cost of orthodontic treatment, the best approach is to use a promissory note signed by the patient.

For example, when I first took my eldest child to a local orthodontist, the doctor presented me with the total cost. He then asked me to see the business office manager regarding how I would make payment. The manager and I agreed on a payment plan. She then filled out a piece of paper and asked me to sign it. It was the most frightening document I was ever asked to sign. It said, in effect, that I agreed to pay this amount of money each month for X months beginning now, for a total payment, without interest, of such and such.

The cruncher came in the next paragraph, which said that if I missed even one payment, when due, the entire balance was then due and I was liable for court costs and any attorney fees that the doctor may incur as a result of proceeding against me to collect.

I looked at the form and said, "Do you really expect me to sign that?" I thought her response was classic. She said, "Oh, Mr. Sklar, we're not worried about you. We know the kind of work you do and where you live in this area. You're a respected member of the community and the last person we'd expect a payment problem from. (I already knew I was in trouble. You can tell when your shtick is being used against you!) But, I think you'd agree that even in Burlingame, California, there are a few people who're less than honest, wouldn't you?" I agreed. She continued, "It's because of those people—because there are always a few bad apples in every barrel—that we have to do this. Obviously, you intend

to keep the agreement we just made. I have no doubt of that."
She then handed me the pen.

I took it, and I signed. What else could I do! For me to refuse signing would be admitting that I might possibly be one
of those bad apples she spoke about. And since I intended to
keep the agreement, what harm would there be in accepting
a penalty for welshing on a deal?

I call her technique "hanging a millstone of responsibility
on someone's head." If the person tries to wiggle out, he reveals himself as a potential problem in paying as agreed.

An important consideration for doctors' offices is whether
the doctor should quote fees or get involved in payment arrangements. I think that the doctor can either tell the patient
the total fee for the work done or fill out the codes that enable the staff to quote the charge. Either way, the staff should
be left to discuss how the fee will be taken care of. There are
exceptions of course, such as dentists who are good at presenting not only the total cost of the treatment plan but in
discussing the options available for payment.

If the patient asks the doctor directly for a break in how
the bill is going to be paid, the doctor should say that he always delegates that matter to his staff so that he's free to
concentrate on providing the best treatment and he doesn't
have to compromise that treatment in any way with payment considerations.

The doctor should set the policy and let the staff implement it. The minute the doctor starts giving dispensations,
the word passes to others, and the staff is undermined. Suppose one patient hears about a special payment arrangement
made with a friend and wants the same deal. The response,
in general, is, "When you, patient, are in the same situation,
we can talk about it."

If a staff member is trying to collect and the patient wants
to talk to the doctor about it, the response should be, "As you
know, Doctor is happy to talk with his patients about anything relating to the practice. When it comes to payment of
fees, though, he'll refer you to me, so why don't you and I try

to work this out?" You aren't refusing to let the patient see the doctor; you're just trying to avoid wasted motion.

All these ideas represent quite a bit of change for most healthcare offices. To get started and keep the ball rolling, I recommend *regular* office staff meetings. Hardly any office has them; yet they're invaluable. Communication about financial matters must be forced, and meetings with doctor(s) must be scheduled. The agenda can rotate among the participants. The person who conducts the meetings should also be changed each time. If the boss runs all the meetings, few other people participate.

Finally, I hope people from other businesses who are reading this book make the obvious connection that when I say "doctor," just substitute the word "boss."

———————

Conclusion: These are fast-changing times, and healthcare is among the fastest-changing businesses. You'll be a victim only if you allow it to happen. Take charge of change.

23

Special Collection Challenges in Other Industries

Some businesses enforce collection with heart-stopping measures. A businessman who doesn't repay the loan shark may find his store torched. The gambler who can't pay the debt can expect to spend time in a hospital nursing broken fingers or limbs. Those who cheat their drug dealers don't have a long life expectancy.

These grisly examples illustrate several points, one of which is that almost all businesses, legitimate or not, have collection problems. Even the most loudly trumpeted announcement of horrible consequences for nonpayment doesn't prevent some debtors from welshing on their agreements to pay.

There's no surefire way to guarantee payment. Even home mortgage payments are experiencing 7 percent to 9-1/2 percent delinquency (thirty days or more overdue), with 1 percent of the loans in the process of foreclosure. On the other hand, you don't have to make it easy for debtors to rip you off. Nor do you want to make doing business with you so difficult that you encourage customers to go elsewhere or do without. In this chapter, I summarize the key concepts useful for businesses, consumer or commercial, as they strive to reduce the losses from nonpayment or slow payment and also increase their sales.

In many businesses, a written agreement is essential; in others, it's impossible or impractical. Following is a simple agreement for legal services. It leaves no obvious room for misunderstanding and provides maximum leverage for guaranteeing payment. I've underlined the key payment ideas, and I've made personal comments in parentheses.

FAMILY RELATIONS RETAINER AGREEMENT

1. You have retained the office of Kettle and Black, Counselors at Law, as your attorneys in connection with this proceeding between you and your spouse in the Superior Court of the State of California.

2. We will engage in negotiations concerning, and if necessary, will litigate, the following items and others that might arise, on your behalf:

Spousal support

Property division

Attorney's fees and costs

Tax consequences

Enforcement of Orders

3. You understand at present that *it is impossible to determine precisely the nature and extent of the necessary legal services in your matter.* (No guarantees are made.) To minimize attorney's fees and to preserve as friendly a relationship as possible between you and your spouse, we will try to effect an amicable settlement between you and your spouse. You understand, however, that settlement efforts may not succeed and that it may be necessary to litigate, in which event our fees will be higher.

4. You agree to pay to the firm of Kettle and Black a fee for ser-

vices at an hourly rate. The hourly rate to be charged to you shall be as follows:

$150.00 per hour for the services of Charles Kettle

$135.00 per hour for the services of Lisa Black

$100.00 per hour for the services of Arthur Pott

As we have agreed, Lisa Black shall be the primary attorney handling your case.

The hourly rate shall include, but is not limited to, travel to and from court and/or depositions, negotiations, drafting and reviewing of agreements, document review and preparation, consultations, correspondence, in-office preparation for court proceedings and depositions, discovery by way of interrogatories, admissions, or other discovery devices, legal research, and telephone conversations. (With this definition, you can charge for thinking time.)

5. As we have agreed, you are to pay a retainer amount of $1000.00. (It's great when you can get money up front.) The retainer is due and payable with the return of the retainer agreement. We do bill against the retainer until it is depleted, and then you shall receive a monthly bill that is to be paid within thirty (30) days of receipt. You agree to pay us the difference between the total fee and the retainer paid.

6. We shall render monthly statements to you, indicating the current status of your account, both for services rendered and for out-of-pocket disbursements on your behalf. These statements shall be due and payable upon receipt. If payment is not made and your monthly statement exceeds $1000.00, this office shall have the option of either withdrawing from your case or suspending work on your case until your account is brought current. Interest on the unpaid balance shall be added at the rate of 1.0% per month commencing thirty (30) days after billing. (Losses are cut, and the interest discourages slow payment.)

7. Independent of the fee arrangement under paragraph 4, you agree to pay the out-of-pocket disbursements such as filing fees, subpoena costs, deposition costs, long distance telephone calls, accounting fees, investigation costs, process server costs, photocopying charges, travel expenses, and all similar charges. (Don't expect us to absorb these costs.)

8. The provisions of this agreement with respect to the fee

arrangement will be disclosed to the court in connection with any application by us for fees for services we render on your behalf. We shall also advise the court of any amount we receive on account.

9. We shall not make any settlement or institute court proceedings without your consent.

10. We shall have the right to withdraw from your case if you do not make the payments required by this agreement (see number 6 above), if you have misrepresented or failed to disclose material facts, or if you fail to follow our advice. In any of those events, you shall execute a substitution of attorneys form at our request. (You should now know who's in control.)

11. We shall have a lien on all your documents, property, or money in our possession for the payment of all sums due us from you under this agreement. (As you can see, we're very serious about getting paid.)

12. If it is necessary for us to file suit for the collection of any sums due us from you under this agreement, you shall pay reasonable attorney's fees together with court costs for their collection.

13. You acknowledge that we have made no guarantees regarding the disposition of any phase of this matter and all expressions relative to it are only our opinions as attorneys.

14. There is no change or waiver of any of the provisions of this agreement unless the change is in writing and signed by you and a member of our firm. It is understood that a waiver or change of any part of this agreement does not constitute a waiver or change of any other part, unless expressly stated.

I have read the foregoing agreement and agree to all the terms and conditions herein and acknowledge receipt of a copy of this agreement.

Dated: _____   Dated: _____
                                    Kettle and Black
                                    Counselors at Law

By: _____   By: _____
                                    Lisa Black

Driver's License No.: _____
Social Security No.: _____

Here's a much simpler agreement by the same law firm for representing a business client:

Date:

Re:

Dear:

Thank you for giving this firm the opportunity to represent you. We welcome the opportunity to be of service to you.

For your information, please be advised of the following:

1. Mr. Kettle will bill at the rate of $175.00 per hour,
2. Mr. Pott will bill at the rate of $100.00 per hour,
3. Telephone calls will be billed starting at a minimum of one-quarter of an hour,
4. Court costs, long-distance telephone calls, and excess photo-copying will be billed to your account.

Please be advised that your account will be charged a 1 percent handling charge if payment is not made within a thirty-day (30 days) period. Furthermore, if payment is not made and your monthly statement exceeds $1000.00, this office shall have the option of either withdrawing from your case or suspending work on your case until your account is brought current.

In addition, if at any time it becomes necessary for us to file suit for the collection of any sums due this firm, you will be responsible for paying reasonable attorney's fees, including court costs.

As we discussed, we will require a retainer in the amount of $1000.00, which is to be returned with the signed original of this contract letter. An envelope has been provided for your convenience. The copy is for your records. The original will then be placed in your file because the State Bar of California requires your written consent to the terms and conditions outlined above before we can represent your interests and handle your case.

Once again, thank you for choosing our firm.

Sincerely,

Kettle and Black, Counselors at Law

I agree to the above:

Company name	Address

Federal tax I.D. number	City, state, zip code

By: _____   _____
                                   Driver's license number
Individual
By: _____   _____
Name   Social security number

_____   _____
Address   Driver's license number

_____
City, state, zip code

Key Concepts

Point 1: Get Money Up Front If You Can

Deposits of any kind are helpful. For apartment rentals, the landlord insists on the first and last month's rent plus a security deposit.

When you reserve a hotel room for late arrival, the hotel asks for your credit card number so they're sure they won't lose money on the room for that night. To hold a meeting at a hotel, you have to sign an agreement and perhaps pay a deposit. The agreement provides the basis for charging if you do have the meeting. The deposit gives the hotel some financial comfort in case you decide to cancel the meeting (which happens frequently).

Hotels constitute a curious type of credit grantor. Their main business is selling sleeping rooms. As with airplanes, if the space isn't used, the revenue is lost forever. When you arrive to get your room, they're cold-blooded (but friendly) about getting paid before giving you your room key. First the room clerk asks for your credit card and then imprints it.It's not that hotels don't trust you. It's just that there's no reason why they should. You can, however, negotiate room rates. A business traveler should ask for the commercial rate. You may get it even if you don't ask, but why run the risk?

Hotels are much more flexible about meeting rooms. If you can guarantee a block of, say, fifty sleeping rooms, you can usually get the meeting room free. But I digress. Even though collecting includes the need to negotiate, let's return to some of the other collection damage control points for most businesses.

Point 2: Control the Money Flow If You Can

The agreements collection agencies usually have with their clients include the commission to be paid on moneys collected. Most debtors pay the agency, which then takes out its commission and remits the balance to the client. But many debtors pay the client directly, and some of those clients deny that they were paid. Because it would be terribly embarrassing for a collection agency to admit that it couldn't collect on the commission owed for such client payments, most agencies have a provision in their agreements that allow them to "offset" the money for the direct payment to the client against the net owed to the client for the other payments made by the client's debtors to the agency.

Another example of a business that controls the money flow is the agreement that agents have with authors of books that requires all royalty payments to flow from the publisher to the agent, who then takes his percentage before mailing the balance of the royalty to the author. Authors would prefer that the publisher pay them directly, but then the agent would be stuck with having to collect from the writer, if that were the arrangement.

Point 3: Get Credit History and Payment Information

Asking a new customer for a large amount of credit information has two benefits. One is the value of having as much information as possible for establishing the amount of credit that's reasonable and for potential skiptracing of assets and/or locating a skipped debtor.

The second advantage is psychological: The more credit information a debtor reveals, the less likely it is that the debtor will be tempted to default, or default as much, as quickly, or with as many phony excuses.

Be cautious with credit when you set up a new business customer, even if the credit report shows positive indicators. As mentioned in a previous chapter, the information on many Dun & Bradstreet reports is provided by the business owner; Dun & Bradstreet guarantees no independent verification.

When a business supplies three credit references, they're obviously giving you the names of three businesses they pay promptly, probably because they have to have those products or services. You must look for how your new customer will be paying *you*. That will take time to establish, so start cautiously with credit.

The growing defaults on student loans constitute a prime example of multiple collection follies: insufficient credit information, poor tracking of debtors after graduation, policy conflicts, not enough effort to collect, plus the added insult of doctors and lawyers who become wealthy and refuse to pay off the loans that gave them the education to generate that wealth. The picture becomes lurid when we see an occasional Cadillac or Rolls being towed away by a government that occasionally gets tough (and gets the picture in the paper) to make a point.

Point 4: Cut Your Losses

Folk wisdom holds that the best loss is the first loss. That bit of hardscrabble insight applies as much to cutting your losses in a declining stock as it does to managing your nonperforming accounts receivable. I believe that a decision to stop nursing unpaid accounts after three to five months provides a number of benefits. The obvious one is that you stop wasting time, time that could be expended with far greater cash flow results on the newer accounts. You also experience less stress when you work on accounts that have a greater probability of paying.

What isn't so obvious is that when you recognize accounts older than three to five months as not worth your time and money to collect, the admission is psychologically painful in that it implies failure in both policy and collection skills, neither of which reinforces one's positive self-image. But the willingness to face the truth and to accept the inevitable errors in judgment and execution, although debilitating on the surface, have a salutary effect on future policy and action. Specifically, they force the business to adopt more professional policies, to issue clearer communications, and to be more consistent about policy within the company.

The reverse is the norm for most businesses; they don't bite the bullet on slow-paying accounts for nine months to a year, or longer. This laissez-faire attitude masks the casualness of the credit and collection policy as well as guaranteeing a higher level of accounts receivable. The willingness to cut one's losses early provides benefits to a business and only one penalty, which is that one's pride gets nicked a bit.

You can cut your losses before you do business, particularly with purchases paid by check. If your business does much business by check, you're probably familiar with check authorization/protection companies such as Telecheck, Telecredit, and others. Telecredit, for example, processes more than 50 million check transactions a year, valued at $8 billion in purchases. Since some of those checks go bad, Telecredit paid $80,000,000 to the merchants who used the service, or about 1 percent of the total check amount guaranteed. For this service, the merchant pays 1/2 percent to 5 percent of the check value, which is in the range of the cost for offering credit card sales.

Credit cards are accepted and check guarantee services are used for the same reasons: to increase sales while minimizing the collection losses from those sales—up front. Check guarantee services aren't for everyone; in small towns, the need is less compelling. Still, only 4 percent of the merchants who could benefit from check guarantee services are doing so. Many merchants resist paying the cost of the service as though it were a loss, whereas, on balance, the profit from the added sales tends to make use of the service a sound business decision.Once again, the fear of loss rears its ugly head. However, check guarantee services are a dandy way to minimize the loss from, and the risk of, bad checks.

Public utilities have a charming way of enforcing payment policies: They issue a warning or two and then cut off the phone service or the power (exceptions are made in the colder parts of the country). In spite of this awesome collection power, utilities have immense collection problems and use outside collection services extensively. For many years, utilities exhibited the mind-set of many businesses with regard to collection. Because utilities are a public service organization, serving the public was drummed into the heads of all employees.

Pressing for payment seems to be in direct conflict with a service mentality, and utilities in many parts of the country have been slow to develop their own in-house collection departments or enforce clear-cut policies and early write-offs.

The utilities' collection problems are illuminating. Many businesses with no recourse wish they had the power to shut off their essential services as a way to prod for payment. But as you can see, even that power, when squandered, doesn't do the utility much good.

As you go about the business of cutting your losses, plan different actions for accounts based on dollar amount, assets, cost to collect, and value of the customer for future business. For accounts of, say, $50 or less, two letters from you plus two more from an outside precollection letter service may be all you should do. With larger accounts, make a phone call or two, and use an attorney, a small-claims court, or a collection agency if you're getting nowhere.

Point 5: Create Urgency

Never mind that your customer has other bills to pay, has lost his job, or is facing some other disaster. Even with all the money in the world, any consumer or business can easily make a wish list of other expenditures they'd prefer or prioritize current bills, with yours nowhere near the top. Either way, you have to fight for your money, whether your customer is an unknown or a close friend. In fact, having a close friend for a customer often produces stress when your friend presumes you don't need to be paid so fast.

Urgency is the antidote to complacency. There's never enough money for your customers to pay all their bills on time. So, unfortunately, the squeaky wheel gets the grease; you'd better squeak early and often.

Debtors will test you in ways both subtle and gross, but the result will be the same: You won't get paid. The stratagems will range from pleading for your understanding to complete indifference when you say you'll sue. The possibilities remind me of Father Damien in *The Exorcist* when he explained that the Devil comes in all forms, even that in the form of the protective mother. Your debtors can likewise assume infinite guises if they so wish. Whatever type of business you're in, you're dealing with other human beings. Your understanding of what makes people tick gives you the edge in selling and collecting.

Whenever there's a possibility of a misunderstanding about payment, you can expect customers to misunderstand, in their favor. Even when you spell it all out, you don't eliminate the problem. If you don't normally see your customers, as in a telephone answering service, send your payment policy in the mail and have it returned, signed. If you're a plumber tired of proving how long you were on the job, ask the customer to sign or initial the piece of paper that shows exactly when the job started and when it ended.

If a landscaping or building design service produces a plan that can be executed by others, and the service expects to be paid for the design regardless, that provision had better be spelled out in advance and signed for. In a tenuously related example, for years advertising agencies have spent hundreds of thousands of dollars preparing presentations of new advertising campaigns, on speculation, in competition with several competitors, with no guarantee of getting the business and with a clear understanding that the prospect doesn't pay for the cost of the planning and presentation.

Recently, some agencies have refused to do this work without more certainty that their efforts would be rewarded. This isn't a collection problem, but it's close. It has to do with the willingness to cut one's losses while risking losing the business. The quality of that decision is comparable to the decision to press a key customer, albeit a slow paying one, to stop taking your business for granted in how it pays you.

Conclusion: Industries differ. Businesses within an industry also vary in their policies and positioning. What doesn't vary so much are the fears, attitudes, and policies of the people in these businesses as they affect their success or failure in collecting.

24

Collection Checklist—A Consultant's Guide to Curing the Problem

____

Would you like to *do something* about your business policies and procedures for credit and collection? This chapter is a blueprint for action, a collection checklist. You can use it in your own business, or use it to consult for others.

Of necessity, the checklist is general; different industries can add and delete as necessary. Systematic use of the collection checklist becomes a productive act by focusing on the problem, by acknowledging its existence, by implying that changes for the better can be made.

When you work with the checklist, the participants are in a position to think about policies that, in many cases, have been in place for a while and were appropriate for conditions that existed at an earlier time. But conditions change. The market changes. The nature of competition changes. Your business goals may change. People in the company change. However, your business policies, specifically your credit and collection policies, may not have changed or changed enough. We resist change, sometimes with good reason.

Therefore, the checklist provides a useful exercise in examining how you operate. You can only benefit from the process; there's no downside.

The people affected by the checklist study almost always welcome the opportunity to contribute their thoughts about the policies they have to administer. They definitely have opinions about those policies. Many of these people will be delighted to have the opportunity to question policies, give reasons, and recommend changes. After all, the people in the trenches do have a unique point of view that can add understanding to the data that measure their activities.

When I consult, I use a two-part survey. Part 1, which follows, is filled out and returned to me before I show up. If you're analyzing your own business, you can have the credit and collection people prepare part 1.

One person in the business office is the designated writer, and everyone participates in crafting the answers to each question. Some of the questions will stimulate debate, argument, or a need to look up the data; all these activities are useful.

Part 1

Following are the types of questions used in part 1. Provide enough space for answers to these questions. Modify the questions for your business as needed.

1. Who is participating in this survey?
2. How would you describe the business?
3. Main sources of customers?
4. How many customers a day (or month) by each source of business?
5. How many bills are sent each month?
6. How often are accounts receivable aged? Attach a copy of most recent aging.

7. How well does your billing and collecting system meet your needs?
8. What credit information do you get, and how do you use it?
9. What debtor payment excuses give you the most trouble?
10. Who does the billing? Collecting?
11. What specific goals would you like to achieve in collecting?
12. What specific areas in your collections would you like to improve on, solve, avoid, feel more comfortable with, etc?
13. Any other comments you would like to make?
14. Who prepared this evaluation?

As you can see, the information produced from part 1 gives the consultant plenty of information about attitudes, policies, goals, and areas of weakness.

The consultant will use this information to probe, using the question *why* frequently. Draw out the participants: Why did you chose this collection goal? Why do you feel your present system is inadequate? Please be specific. Is Dave the best person to make collection phone calls? Why?

Part 2

Part 2 of the checklist is filled out by the consultant, or by you if you're evaluating your own company.

1. Present Payment Policy
   a. What is your policy on quoting prices on the phone?
   b. How much payment do you ask for when product/ service is delivered/ordered?
   c. What is your policy on multiple payments?
   d. Do you use interest, cash discount, charge cards, terms?
   e. Policy for special orders?

    f. Policy for new customers?

2. Present Billing and Collecting System
   a. Manual or other system used?
   b. How often are customers billed?
   c. Messages used on statements?
   d. When are collection phone calls made? How? By whom? What followup is done?
   e. When you do bite the bullet? What alternatives do you use? How effective have they been for you?
   f. Do you ever "fire" customers?
   g. What is current measure of collection effectiveness?
   h. How, exactly, do you ask for payment?
   i. What is the boss's role in asking debtors for payment or handling customers with payment problems?
   j. How do you use your accounts receivable aging report? What are your goals for your receivables?
   k. How often do you review difficult-to-collect accounts? What is the review process?
   l. Is there any incentive for improved collections?
   m. How often do you hold staff meetings?
   n. Would you be willing to lose some customers or forego some future business to reach your collection goals?

I promise you that a discussion of these questions will stimulate a lively discussion, hopefully leading to insight, change, and commitment.

If you take the consultant's role, you don't tell a business what its policy should be; that is a subjective matter unique to each business. Your role is to illuminate issues in a way that the business can more clearly define what policies it wants for itself. You can then be a guide on how best to communicate those policies to customers and those within the organization.

Conclusion: You care enough about your company's collections to read this book. Now dive in, grab your collection policy by the throat, and make some changes.

25

Training Collectors: How to Hire, Train, Motivate, Retain

Training collectors involves a certain set of problems: Where do you get the people, how do you train them, who trains them, how can you motivate them, and how do you keep them? Before we start solving these problems, let's look at them more closely, beginning with the notion that you can't get enough qualified collectors.

We already know that job candidates don't fight to become collectors, thanks to low job status, limited earning potential (unless a commission plan is available), minimal opportunities for advancement and, in many companies, a limited commitment to training. Even professional collection agencies constantly whine that they can't get enough good collectors; they create a dual path to despair that goes like this: All the good collectors that we don't already have work for someone else, and we don't want to hire them and have to break the bad habits ingrained in them from other companies. Our alternative is to hire new recruits, off the street, and train them, but we don't have enough time, and even if we did, we'd just be training them to go to work somewhere else.

What a negative attitude. This is a classic example of seeing a glass half empty instead of half full, of expecting guarantees instead of being willing to take chances and play the percentages. Since I know and have worked with hundreds of collection agencies and their owners for the past twenty years, I can assure you that the sour attitude just described is realistic for many agency owners. If collection agency professionals, who usually pay salary plus commission, bemoan the ease of getting good people, you can conclude that other businesses, whose main business isn't collecting, have an even tougher time getting and keeping quality collectors, and you're right.

But It Doesn't Have to Be That Way

Collectors can be given the status, training, career path, and compensation comparable to that offered the salespeople. I realize that most companies suffer from a troubling turnover in salespeople, but that never seems to diminish the awareness of salespeople's importance and the need for deploying good ones.

Here I present concrete steps to take to enable your collectors to contribute more to the bottom line, to feel better about themselves and their chosen careers, and help you reduce turnover.

Elevate Status and Create a Career Path

Status is a quirky matter. You don't wave a wand at a job function and announce that henceforth this job now has status. Status can change. In earlier times, actors had miserable status, but today we envy movie stars and even news anchors. The schoolmarm of yesteryear and the college professor once enjoyed a special respect in the community. Today, we may experience a twinge of condescension for those noble but slightly frayed pursuits—at least in economic terms.

Status has its ups and downs. The good news, then, is that you may be able to change the status of collectors. One way is to change the label. Garbage collectors have become "sanitation engineers," employees are now "associates," and housewives are called "household managers." Some of this language change is done tongue-in-cheek, but it does contribute to changing attitudes.

For example, a few decades ago, some people in this country persisted in the notion that black people were inherently inferior and should be treated as such. Black leaders realized that this assumption couldn't be allowed to go unchallenged if changes were to be made, so "Black is beautiful" emerged as a countervailing theme to rally the troops. The phrase, the attitude, and the commitment behind the slogan all combined to produce changes in legislation against discrimination and even some attitude changes between the races.

The point is that status can be changed. An easy beginning is a job title change from collector to Account Manager, Account Analyst, Collection Analyst, or any other fancy-sounding job title. Labels are important because they confer status. In Japan, when Japanese businessmen meet foreigners, they first exchange business cards so that, depending on the job title, the Japanese host will know how low to bow. Other simple but effective ways to proclaim status include:

1. Provide an attractive office and office furniture. Prepare business cards for each employee.
2. Invest in collection technology that improves the efficiency as well as the status of the accounts analysts.
3. Provide recognition awards—the more the merrier. Surveys repeatedly show that people value recognition

and appreciation way above compensation regarding job satisfaction.

4. Make training and seminars available on a regular basis. Your willingness to invest the time and money speaks loudly and also pays off in more skilled and eager people.
5. Subscribe to credit and collection trade publications.
6. Proclaim the value of collectors to the company's well-being. Let everyone in the company know it, and give examples in concrete, economic terms.
7. Develop a career path that has the best job candidates fighting to join your company.

Provide a Career Path

1. Let new hires know in advance what opportunities exist in personal growth, job advancement, and compensation, both direct and indirect.
2. Create a sequence of job responsibilities, going from trainee to business analyst, that increases at each step the job responsibility, pay, perks, and benefits.
3. Have regular office meetings that include the accounts analysts.
4. Commit to ongoing training and seminars.
5. Have present staff develop the training manual and the training course. Continue to improve both. Make your training course a key weapon in hiring and motivating because that's exactly what it is. Few businesses will take time away from their day-to-day activities to develop these materials. But if you've got it, flaunt it.

Become Creative in Hiring

Hiring is usually done through newspaper ads. Most ads are

similar in that they highlight the job requirements the business is looking for and then make it clear that they'll consider an applicant who's energetic, eager to learn, and grateful for the opportunity. I've always received more and better applicants by appealing to what the job seeker is looking for. I don't omit describing the job, but the focus is on

1. Pleasant people to work with
2. Great opportunity to learn, grow, be appreciated
3. Interesting work, leading to advancement

Aren't these what people really want—what you want?

If you use newspaper ads for hiring, place your ad in several categories in the classified section. Put the main ad under Accounts Receivable Specialist. Put small ads under General Office, Collectors, Credit and Telemarketing categories that say, "See our ad for Accounts Receivable Specialist," plus your company name.

I'm not going to discuss techniques to use in the interview process because so much good material on that subject is already available. I do suggest, as part of the interview, that you let the applicant listen to a collector work to see how he or she feels about the work. I'd like to comment on an interesting, seldom-used, and very effective technique that greatly increases the odds of hiring winners. I have fun with business owners when I ask them this question: "If there were a way of knowing, in advance, before you hire someone, how the person was going to turn out on the job, would you like to know about it?" I always get an emphatic "Yes!"

There is a way; it's called graphology, or handwriting analysis. Many people, particularly hard-nosed businesspeople, tend to put graphology in the same light as fortune telling or astrology. But that's a mistake. I can tell you from personal experience how to use a professional handwriting analyst to greatly improve the odds in the hiring process. (Note that I said "improve the odds"; I said nothing about guarantees.) Graphology is like collecting and selling—you use it to improve the odds in your favor. If you're expecting 100 percent certainty, don't look for it on this planet.

Your job candidate fills out the usual application and also writes some narrative, in ink, about some question you pose. In your application, let the applicant know that the information given may be used for handwriting analysis. The professional graphologist will serve several useful purposes, including

1. Screening out those applicants who'd be obvious misfits.
2. Helping you learn about hidden qualities in good candidates. This knowledge will enable you to work even better with them, even though you might have hired them without using graphology.

In job interviews, all candidates put their best foot forward. The resumes are sparkling and the reference letters glowing. Wouldn't it be better to know the real people behind the mask? The situation is analogous to two people who get married. No matter how much time people spend together prior to marriage, it seems that they get to know all of the other person only after they get hitched.

Newspaper ads are not the only venue for spreading the word about the job openings; there are four other possibilities:

1. Determine if present clerical personnel have the aptitude, interest, and potential.
2. Offer present employees a bounty for finding applicants among their friends and friends' friends. One bounty program offered $20 for an applicant who'd be worth interviewing, an additional $50 if the applicant was hired, another $50 if the applicant stayed on the job for a month, plus a final $50 after six months.
3. Put notices on supermarket bulletin boards where allowed.
4. Call your collection agency, if you have one. Ask them to refer to you any of their applicants who are good but don't meet their job requirements. If you have no

agency, offer one some of your business in exchange for its help in finding people.

Be Serious About Training

In far too many businesses, training is a joke, considered nonproductive, or maybe productive long term. The irony is that the benefits yield more than the knowledge gained from the training. The sheer attention the employee receives helps generate a feeling of loyalty to the company.

Some business owners also begrudge training because they feel that they're training employees for the benefit of some other company. If they have a high volume of turnover, those feelings are understandable, but the problem can be corrected.

A collector training manual should include, at minimum:

1. Company policy on credit and collection
2. Restatement of the career path and the importance of collections to the business's well-being
3. Rules on harassment as defined by the Federal Fair Debt Collection Practices Act
4. Information on other relevant legislation, such as the Federal Fair Credit Reporting Act
5. Skiptracing policy, resources, and techniques
6. Telephone techniques
7. Written messages you use
8. How to resolve accounts
9. Steps to take when account cannot be collected economically
10. Collection procedures, abbreviations, number and types of accounts, measurements of performance, and goals for this business

In addition to the course training material, plenty of time

should be devoted to role playing. As you know, it's my favorite method of accelerating learning or, for that matter, more quickly weeding out people who really shouldn't be working as collectors. Either result is valuable.

Training should be an ongoing activity. Use outside seminars. Bring trainers in, if your staff is large enough or if you have a big collection problem that needs to be attacked from a fresh point of view. If someone attends a collection seminar, have them report the next day or at the next office meeting what they learned and what specific measures the company should consider taking as a result.

Stay Current on Technology

Technology has come to the collection field with a vengeance, and its impact on productivity is phenomenal. I've always believed that one-time capital investments provide much more profit than continually paying for too many people or for people who aren't as efficient as they can be. Collection technology today includes:

1. Cardless computer systems. These systems eliminate the need to handle hard copy accounts media and save time wasted filing and unfiling hard copy media as well as losing them.
2. Automatic phone dialing systems. The goal is to have the collector spend as much time as possible in phone negotiation with debtors. These systems typically send out all the written communications either automatically or when the collector triggers them.
3. Automated access to directory information at the phone company.
4. Direct access to credit reports.
5. Hands-free headsets. Collectors can speak into a device while their hands are free for other work.

6. Ergonomic (comfortable) chair, good lighting, nonglare monitor screen, a no-smoking area, background music.

The technology to handle the clerical scutwork is expanding rapidly.

Another vital consideration in account management is the number of accounts a collector has to work on. Most businesses put too many accounts in the hands of each collector.How many is too many? With a manual system, 1000 accounts is plenty but 750 would be even better. With automation, you can easily increase that number.

Technology won't help in a crucial component of account management: the decision criteria used to stop working on accounts. That's a matter of policy, judgment, and guts. The policy should consider the size, age, and number of contacts on an account in determining where to draw the line. When in doubt, stop trying to collect and devote the energy to the more obviously collectible, newer accounts.

Motivate and Retain People

Motivation is tricky business. It's not something you do to someone. You can provide a work environment that encourages people to strive to do their best to motivate themselves. Our earlier ideas on training and career pathing will help produce an upbeat atmosphere, ensuring that those people who do want to do well and be recognized for it will have every opportunity to succeed.

I've read about and tried many motivational ideas, including simple, steady appreciation, sending people to est and similar "awareness" training, regular staff meetings, 5-15 reports each Friday—you name it, we'll give it serious consideration. The 5-15 report is a Silicon Valley-spawned idea whereby each employee, every Friday, turns in a three-part report that takes no more than 5 minutes to read or more than 15 minutes to write. Part 1 concerns what the person did and didn't do this week. Part 2 discusses the person's morale and the morale of others. Part 3 presents an idea for improving things.

Some of the staff grumbles a little about doing the 5-15's each week, but I find them invaluable for three reasons:

1. They allow people to express in writing a problem or a complaint that they wouldn't tell their boss face to face.
2. Yield some great ideas. Most deal with productivity, marketing, and other strictly business functions, but other ideas have resulted in a television in the lunch room and repainting of walls.
3. Provide a more frequent update on who's swamped, who needs more to do, and who's ready to learn something new.

I've even used Art Friedman's policy for compensating employees. Art is a friend and a member of my company's board of directors who observed that most employees don't work as hard or as selflessly as do entrepreneurs and founders of companies.He decided that the reason isn't the employee's fault; the employer causes it by setting wages and granting increases. The problem is that most employees feel unappreciated and definitely underpaid. Naturally, they aren't going to exert their best effort until management pays them what they're worth, and, whatever that is, it's not enough. The attitude is much like that of slaves on a slave ship: Don't row.

To cut through all that clutter, each employee must be allowed to decide personally what she or he is worth. Employees never have had the chance to do that. When they do have the opportunity, they invariably give themselves less than a boss would. People are tough on themselves. They know, blindly, that the boss undervalues them, but when given the freedom to set their own salary, they usually undervalue themselves.

Friedman also lets each employee increase his or her salary for any reason, in any amount, at any time! At this point you may be certain that Art is mad. What happens, however, is that he usually has to push people to take more money.

Most people respond to this nice-sounding theory with the question, "What if the employee wants $10,000 a week" [or some other ridiculous compensation]? The answers are: (1) They won't, and (2) even if they did, you can always fire them. To add to the program's gutsiness, the boss must always assure the employee that whatever is asked for, the boss will agree to.

When I heard about the idea from Art, it sounded crazy, even though I knew he owned a long-established successful appliance business. I thought it over for six months and then finally tried it with one manager. It worked great, so I expanded the idea to all employees. I offered new employees a starting salary only. After a week to a month or more—however long it took to see that the employee was ready for an increase—I called them into my office and told them that they were doing a good job and deserved more money. How much did they want?

As you can imagine, I got some incredulous reactions. Some asked me what the going rate was. I told them but added that that rate may not be right for them; I always put the burden back on them to decide. Some were afraid they'd ask too little. I told them they could always increase it. I explained the concept, and they still struggled to name a figure. Imagine! You have an opportunity to name your own compensation, and you struggle over it. One person couldn't do it, but everyone else managed to come up with a figure.

One day, one man asked for more than I thought he was worth. I gave it to him anyway and immediately called Art, who explained that the man will either work himself up to the point where he does deserve that salary or he'll soon force himself to quit, due to the guilt of knowing he's not worth what he's getting. So, taking a leap of faith, I waited.

Sure enough, in about three weeks, the employee showed a new, elevated level of responsibility and productivity.

This theory illustrates how in business we're using little of the lessons learned in other fields of study. The epilogue to the Art Friedman story is that he started a microwave oven store in 1976 and then franchised it. Ninety-five franchisees were offered, and Art didn't have to seek out and sell any of them—they all came to him because of how he deals with people.

Motivation also includes demanding excellence from employees. Ineffective people must be fired. Good people resent working around drones. Just as in collecting an uncollectible account, you need to cut your losses and move on.

Conclusion: One person's problem is another person's opportunity. Your business can get the top-notch collectors it wants, just by applying the ideas in this chapter. It's easy. Trust me.

26

Summing Up and Looking Ahead

Y ou've noticed that I used precious few statistics in this book, which is a bit unusual. This type of book tends to buttress points, whenever possible, by quantifying them. I come from the school that shuns so-called "gee whiz" statistics. Suppose, for example, that you learned that total consumer debt was 150 incredibillion, or corporate write-offs in 1988 totaled 280 million. The numbers may be interesting, may point to the need for some new public policy, and may even raise the hackles of people in some public or private organization enough to get some useful change made. All this is laudable. But the usual results of a statistic-infected article include the reader's eyes glazing over, the article being padded, and purpose skewed toward fact instead of insights.

On the other hand, avoidance of relevant data indicates a lazy writer and a poorly researched article of doubtful usefulness. The point is that (1) overall, statistics don't mean much to an individual businessperson. What's important is how *my* company is doing, are *my* receivables hurting me, do *we* need to change our policy and procedures. (2) Most of the wisdom in collections comes from the psychological arena, the willingness to confront the problems, admit they exist, prepare for and make changes, and be willing to "lose" some.

In business, as in other aspects of life, the denial mechanism is a powerful deterrent to change. Writing about general trends produces a result similar to the truly horrible stories we read about starvation in the sub-Sahara. We react with "ain't it awful," and we may even contribute to aid programs. But when the problem is in your own back yard, your own job, your own business, that's "up close and personal." To quote Samuel Johnson, who said of a man about to be hanged, "It concentrates your mind wonderfully."

That oft-quoted remark is relevant in collections. Put another way, as "Tip" O'Neill, former speaker of the house said, "All politics are local." It's no trick to measure the effects of your present policy on your company's credit and collections. If you have any doubt, your CPA or accountant should provide some answers. The insights in this book were gleaned from twenty years of working with all types of businesses all over the United States. After a while, some themes develop and some immutable truths emerge.

When confronted by the scope of one's collection problems, it's convenient to say "so what?" Other business problems may appear more serious, but they merely have to be dealt with right now. Examples include the manager who quits and has to be replaced, the computer that just ate last week's data and there's no backup, and the big customer who defected to your most hated competitor.

A sense of humor about all this helps, which is why in our collection seminars we make little jokes about all the collection problems common to most businesses, such as the habit of holding on to nonpaying accounts twice as long as necessary. What we get from pointing out the commonality of these problems is the gallows humor, the misery-loves-company, shared-experience syndrome that lets everyone off the hook a bit because it recognizes that no one is in this alone.

Then comes the confrontation, "Are you ready to do something about it?" Some are and some aren't. The shared guilt also produces a short-term support group, not unlike AA or other dependency support groups. These analogies may be stretching too far to embrace the "evils" of dependency on poor collection strategies, but so what. It's change I'm after, not motivation. Several observers have pointed out that seminars are great for a shot in the arm of motivation. I agree. But it's not enough. These shots in the arm, like the seminars given by big-name sales motivators, are useful for maybe three days. After all, how long can your body keep the adrenaline flowing when the stimulus is no longer there?

No, something more constantly, more ruthlessly, more ingeniously productive is needed, and that something is a change in attitudes. For the regular adrenaline fixes, have your regular office meetings. You can do a number of things as you develop your plans for your future credit and collection policies and tactics, as we now discuss:

Make Salespeople's Compensation Be Affected by Sales Dollars Collected, Not Sales Made

In other words, if the dollars aren't collected, the salesperson responsible is hurt financially. Companies that have adopted this posture report that salespeople moan about it, but they discover a new awareness of the company policy and the activities of the business office. Don't let the salesforce think that collections is someone else's problem. I'd also include sales managers in business office meetings.

When Training New Salespeople, Have Them Spend Time in the Business Office

Even if the new people are old pros from sales in another company, they should learn *your* credit and collection policy and procedures. More radically, let them make collection calls; it's good sales training, and they may even enjoy it. The process also tends to bring together what are often two natural enemies, sales and the business office.

Give All Key Employees a Copy of This Book

Make sure employees read the book. They should also make notes of which ideas should be talked about or even implemented at a meeting to be held for that purpose.

Discuss the Credit and Collection Policy at Regular Office Meetings

The boss should participate, at least part of the time. As part of the meeting, discuss current tough accounts so that others can make suggestions about how to handle them. Include a session of role playing so that everyone keeps their skills sharpened.

Look Closely at a New Business Service Called Rent-A-Collector or Collectemps

As the name suggests, this option is available when you have unpaid accounts piling up, you can't afford to write them off, you can't justify adding to your permanent staff to wrestle with a short-term problem, and, above all, you can't afford to ignore the problem since the cost to you increases daily.

The accounts given to Collectemps typically are two to four months old. Accounts older than that should go to one of the bite the bullet choices, such as an outside collection agency. Your inside collection temps will give you a return on investment of $4 to $5 for each dollar invested, or more.

That's a darn good return on investment. To prove it, I'll use an example that you'll have to adjust for your business.

Assume 100 accounts averaging $150, or a total of $15,000, in accounts, say, three months old. Assume also that the temporary collector can handle five accounts an hour, which includes skiptracing, busy signals, live conversations with debtors, recordkeeping, and whatever else has to be done with the account. Further assume that you're going to pay $25 an hour for the temp (I'm using an hourly figure that will challenge your sense of reasonableness). Finally, assume that the temp will collect at least 50 percent of these fresh accounts.

Here's how the assumptions pencil out: $7500 will be collected (50 percent of $15,000 in accounts). At 5 accounts an hour, the 100 accounts will be handled to a conclusion in 20 hours. At $25 an hour, you'll pay $500, and no fringe benefits.$7500 collected at a cost of $500 equals an unbelievable 15:1 return on investment, enough to modify the assumptions and still come up with a winner. These are statistics worth considering.

The problem is where to get the temps. The two logical sources are temporary agencies and collection agencies, but there are difficulties with both sources.

Collection agencies have trouble getting people for the collection desks in the agency, and they're usually reluctant to loan you any of their trained people.

Temporary agencies won't have qualified people available for you, although they may offer you telemarketers or others who are good on the phone, and many temporary agencies don't train applicants; they just place them.

If you have a big problem getting good collection temporaries and enough of them, I offer a ray of hope. A few collection agencies are offering good people as a legitimate marketing ploy, a way to convince you to use their third-party collection services if you aren't a client or a way to retain your business if you are a client.

I think temporary collectors are one of the waves of the

future. After all, in this country, services are among the fastest-growing sectors of our economy, and the temporary business is one of the fastest-growing segments of the service business. I'm so enamored of the potential for collection temporaries that I founded, with a partner and a full-time executive, a temporary collection service in one of the major metropolitan areas in the United States. The demand was instantaneous and client satisfaction enormous. Frankly, it's a kick taking an old traditional business like collections and doing something new and even creative with it.

Government Use of Outside Collectors

Some large government entities are overcoming their reluctance to use outside collectors and are hiring collection agencies and attorneys to help deal with the mind- and staff-boggling mountain of unpaid accounts. In certain areas of scandalous nonpayment, such as government-backed student loans, collection agencies have been used for years, but in nowhere near the degree that they should be. The reasons, as usual, are psychological.

Part of the reluctance is the Not Invented Here (NIH) syndrome, whereby the agencies with the problems hate to admit the magnitude of the problem and, to correct it, prefer to get authorization for more bodies in the agency to handle the problem.

Another reason for the unnecessarily slow growth in the use of outside agencies is that the collection agencies may make the government agency look bad by collecting money that the credit granting-agency couldn't get. Once again, so much for logic. As a result, I'm dubious that state, local, or federal organizations owed fortunes by debtors will use the authority that most have already to hire outside collection agencies to clean up their messes.

CPA and Management Consulting Expertise

As the consolidation of giant CPA and management consulting firms increases, I suspect that some firms will develop credit and collection expertise as a way to help claw their way ahead of their competitors. In a competitive, global marketplace, every advantage helps.

Key Changes

Each reader who owns or manages a business can control a few key changes that will give the greatest possible advantage to the business through its credit and collection practices. First, create and communicate a policy, both internal and external, that serves the purpose of the business. The policy must be clear. At some stage of delinquency, it will be "tough." Second, be willing to "lose"—please. Finally, make collection training and role playing a normal activity in the business.

Implement Insights

You can implement the following insights right away if you wish. (1) Establish your business's payment policy, or your customers will do it for you. (2) Follow up on unpaid accounts sooner. (3) Don't hang on to nonpaying or slow-paying accounts so long. Bite the bullet much more quickly. You can't afford to spend the time nursing losers. (4) Make a darn sight more phone calls. (5) As you make these shifts in attitude, policy, and procedures, you can now confront the person at the party who asks, "What do you do?" and say, confidently, "I'm a business analyst," a "financial psychologist," or even a salesman, all of which are true. No more cowering at the question. From now on, the check *will* be in the mail.

P.S. If you have further questions or would like an in-office seminar, workshop, or collection training session, contact my office at (415) 340-1770.

Appendix—Sample Financial Policy

━━━━━

Here we include a sample financial policy for a hospital. Other businesses may be interested in noting how specific this policy is to their type of operation.

Hospital Business Services

Business Services is responsible for the Accounts Receivable, which in many hospitals, outside of plant and equipment, is the second largest asset of the hospital.

Protect the Assets

There are three assets: receivables, guest relations, and staff. To the extent you neglect one, the others are diminished.

1. Receivables—collect them completely and timely to maintain cash flow
2. Guest relations—nurture and foster within the commu-

nity that image of care and trust through genuineness and excellence of service

3. Staff—train, develop, and promote a winning team that's dedicated, confident, and highly motivated.

Philosophy

It is the expectation that all the patients receiving services are financially responsible for the timely payment of all charges incurred. However, no patient will be refused necessary or emergency care if unable to meet the financial requirements of the hospital.

Procedures: Effective Admissions and Outpatient Surgeries

All scheduled insurance covered by insurance(s) will be verified in advance and benefits estimated. The Insurance Verifier will refer all insurance accounts with benefits less than 80 percent of covered charges, and all self-pay accounts, to the Financial Counselor. The Financial Counselor will request a deposit based on the partial payment policy. If immediate hospitalization is not necessary and the guarantor is unable to comply with the requested deposit, upon approval of the attending physician, the patient may be admitted to the county hospital where funding is available, or the admission may be postponed until such time the deposit can be paid. Patients known to be a financial risk will be required to clear any bad debt account, plus their requested deposit as outlined in the partial payment policy.

The Financial Counselor is responsible for monitoring all in-house accounts and requesting further deposits or establishing a ninety-day (90-day) payment plan.

If the patient is hospitalized as a result of an accident, the hospital requires payment directly from the patient or guarantor who receives care and treatment. The hospital will not become involved with an attorney or insurance claim for payment of the account.

Emergency Admissions

The Financial Counselor will be notified immediately, or on the first working day, of any self-pay admissions through the emergency department. The Insurance Verifier will refer all insurance accounts with benefits authorized at less than 80 percent of covered charges. The Financial Counselor is responsible for contacting the patient/guarantor for a deposit based on the partial payment schedule. If the patient cannot reply with the requested deposit, or a ninety-day (90-day) payment plan, the patient will be assigned possible MIA status and transferred to the county hospital with the approval of the attending physician.

Partial Payment Policy

A partial payment will be *requested* from all patients for their *estimated* portion to pay. No patient will be refused necessary treatment due to inability to pay the requested prepayment. The payment schedule, to be maintained by the Director of Business Services, will be used unless approval for a lesser amount is received from the Director of Business Services or the Administration.

Initial Followup

Service Representatives are responsible for patient and/or insurance contacts necessary to secure payment for services. If after ninety (90) days from date of billing payment is still outstanding and short-term arrangements have not been made, the account will be referred for internal collection efforts.

Internal Collection

The Collection Counselors are responsible for following up accounts referred by the Service Representative. Upon the authorization of the Credit Manager, an internally managed account can be directly assigned to the outside collection agency bypassing the precollection letter series.

External Collection

Precollection letters will automatically be generated for inpatient accounts 120 days after billing and for outpatient accounts 90 days after billing. At the end of this cycle (30 days), accounts will be referred to an outside collection agency and written off the accounts receivable to the collector trial. Exceptions to this practice must be authorized by the Credit Manager.

Specific account balance thresholds for write-off are as follows:

Account Balance	Responsibility
Less than $1,000	Credit Manager
Less than $7,500	Director, Business Services
Greater than $7,500	Vice President/Chief Financial Officer

Minor Balance Write-off

Accounts with a patient balance of $7.00 or less are written off weekly under the authority of the Business Office Supervisor. Crossover accounts with an insurance balance of $15.00 or less will be written off under the authority of the Business Office Supervisor.

Good Will/Administrative Write-offs

Write-offs related to hospital incidents will be written off at the request of the Director of Risk Management. Specific account balance thresholds are as follows:

Account Balance	Responsibility
Less than $10,000	Director, Risk Management and Director, Business Services
Greater than $10,000	Director, Risk Management Vice President/Chief Financial Officer

Settlements on accounts for purposes of good will are authorized as follows:

Account Balance	Responsibility
Less than $500	Assistant Director, Business Services
Less than $1,500	Director, Business Services
Greater than $1,500	Vice President/Chief Financial Officer

Partial Payment Policy Schedule

A partial payment will be requested for all patients for their estimated portion to pay according to the following schedule:

1. Private room difference—full amount for estimated length of stay
2. Outpatient surgeries—full amount
3. Medicare deductible and coinsurance—full amount
4. Normal deliveries—$1600
5. C-section—$3500
6. Admission

  a. Medical—$450/day
  b. Surgical—$450/day plus $2,000
  c. Mental health—$425/day
7. Alcohol/drug rehabilitation—$7,000 (minimum $2,500 on admission, $2,500 on discharge and balance in sixty (60) days)
8. Outpatient—full amount
9. Pharmacy—insurance with drug coverage accepted and billed; cash sales for all other customers

Refunds

Service Representatives are responsible for processing patient refunds when the appropriate payee is determined. Specific refund thresholds are as follows:

Credit Balance	Responsibility
Less than $1,000	Supervisor, Business Office
Less than $5,000	Assistant Director, Business Services
Less than $7,500	Director, Business Services
Greater than $7,500	Vice President/Chief Financial Officer

Supervising Your Collections

A supervisor's role of overseeing his or her collectors is vital to the collection process. The supervisor must be able to lead, plan, control, and organize the staff. Example, example, example are the three most important words that can be spoken in the overseeing of the staff. Important points a supervisor should be aware of include the following:

The supervisor should manage by exceptions. What reports does the supervisor have? Does the supervisor have an aged trial balance, particularly by collector, showing the breakdown of the collector's accounts by at least six aging categories?

The supervisor should make sure the collector has all the proper tools and materials, from system access, to policies and procedures, to job description, to goals and objectives, to freedom from burdensome clerical duties, so the collector can actively make calls.

The supervisor should meet regularly with staff to discuss administrative changes, regulatory changes, and department changes.

The supervisor should try to have the collector attend one collection seminar a year and have role-playing exercises at least biannually.

Where possible, a collector's call should be monitored from time to time for appropriate and professional conduct.

Audit, audit, audit. The supervisor should randomly audit a collector's accounts for appropriate and pertinent documentation as well as for timeliness of working the account according to policy and procedure.

The supervisor should be there to support the collector in negotiations. Nothing is more counterproductive than for a collector's decision to be reversed. All questions and problems from the collector should be quickly responded to. Invite feedback; communication is best when it's two-way and frequent.

Take the time to compliment and commend your staff often. Where the environment allows, provide incentive programs for outstanding performance.

Be caring, insist on professional and courteous behavior, and remember that your collection staff is your most important asset. Management is achieving results through others.

For Further Reading

Jules, Charles S. *Beating the Bill Collector Legally.* 1983
Perigree Books-Putnam Publishing Group, 200 Madison
Avenue, New York, NY 10016

Jules supplies good basic information on how debts develop
with major creditors and how they deal with the problem.

Warner, Ralph *Everybody's Guide to Small Claims Court.* 1978
Nolo Press, 950 Parker Street, Berkeley, CA 94710

Warner is a pro at spelling out, in layman language, exactly
how to use "The People's Court." Although the book is
written for California, your county courthouse should be
able to give you the specifics for your state.

Scott, Gini Graham *Debt Collection-Successful Strategies for
the Small Business.* 1987
Oasis Press, 300 North Valley Drive, Grants Pass, OR 97526

This notebook-size manual is strong and detailed on the
methods for suing a debtor. It also includes helpful information on preventing bad debt.

Hardy, Clyde and Martin, Nancy *Your Roles as a Medical
Assistant.* 1974
Medical Economics Company, Oradell, NJ 07649

An excellent guide to all the key roles of a healthcare office staff member, including collections and insurance expert.

Coleman, A. Michael *Advanced Collection Management Handbook: The Art of Getting Paid.* 1988
Coleman and Coleman Consultants, 28 Brookhaven Blvd., Port Jefferson Station, NY 11776

Another notebook-sized manual, Coleman provides a helpful overview of all the elements of credit and collections. Very thorough.

ORDER FORM

Telephone Orders: Call Toll-free (800) 682-8017 [In California, call (415) 340-1770.] Please have your Visa, MasterCard, or Amex card ready.

Postal Orders: Baroque Publishing, 4 West Fourth Avenue, Suite 501, San Mateo, CA 94402.

Please send _____ copy/ies of *The Check Is Not in the Mail*. I understand that I may return it for a full refund, for any reason, no questions asked. **Per copy—$29.95 each**

Sales Tax: Please add 7% for books shipped to California addresses.

Shipping: Book rate: $1.75 for first book and 75 cents for each additional book. Surface shipping may take three to four weeks.

Payment: ☐ Check enclosed (No C.O.D. or PURCHASE ORDERS)
☐ Visa ☐ MasterCard ☐ Amex

Card Number_____ Expires_____

Name on card_____

Ship to:

Name_____

Street Address_____

City/State/Zip_____

Call TOLL-FREE and Order Now

MAIL TO:
Baroque Publishing
4 West Fourth Avenue
Suite 501
San Mateo, CA 94402

JUST FOR FUN

The "end-of-the-world" sign, which is extremely popular at our seminar, is now available to you at a cost of $2.50. The size is 8½" × 11" and is printed in black ink with red flames. Order below.

For Serious Ongoing Training   Leonard Sklar writes a publication, the Sklar Collection Quarterly, that refines your collection strategies, keeps you motivated to carry out your planned improvements, and helps you train others in the company.

Your satisfaction is guaranteed.

To Order
☐ "End of World" sign — $2.50 . . . . ._____
☐ Sklar Collection Quarterly — $32.00 . . . . ._____

TOTAL   _____
(In California add 7% tax)   _____
GRAND TOTAL   _____
(We'll pay shipping and handling)

Order by Phone   Please have credit card available. Call toll-free 1(800)682-8017. In California, call 1(415)340-1770.

Method of Payment (Please Check One)
☐ Cash   ☐ Check
☐ Amex   ☐ Visa   ☐ MasterCard

Card Number_____ Expires_____

Where We Should Send Your Order:

Name_____

Street_____

City/State/Zip_____

Office Phone Number_____

MAIL TO:
Baroque Publishing
4 West Fourth Avenue
Suite 501
San Mateo, CA 94402

THE END OF
THE WORLD
IS COMING!

PLEASE PAY
YOUR BILL SO
WE DON'T HAVE TO
CHASE ALL OVER
HELL
FOR YOU.

COURTESY OF SKLAR SEMINARS

Index

A

Above-the-line debtors,
68–71
Abusive tactics. *See*
Harassment
Accusations of debtors,
144–145
Acknowledgment,
129–131
Address Correction
Requested message,
195
Advertising for collectors,
250–251
Ambulance companies,
223
American Collectors
Association, 124
American Credit
Indemnity, 51
American Express
payments, 55, 56
Amex payments, 55
Amnesty, 62–63
Anesthesiology bills, 218,
219–220
Answering machines. *See*
Phone answering
machines
Asking for money,
105–114
correct techniques for,
111–114
Assessor records on skips,
197
Assets of skips, 199–201
Assignments of benefits,
215–216
Attachment of wages,
144
Attitudes, of collectors,
25–26
Attorneys
customer as, 167–169

Malpractice, medical,
210–211
Management consulting
firms, use of, 263
MasterCard payments, 55,
56
Meaningless promises,
147–149
Medical industry. *See*
Healthcare industry
Medical malpractice,
210–211
Memorial-Sloan Kettering
Hospital, 113
Messages
Address Correction Re-
quested message,
195
Forwarding Postage
Guaranteed mes-
sage, 195
on fourth statement,
80–81
on overdue bills, 80
signs in offices, 88–89
Minors
communication with, 182
phone calls answered
by, 146–147
Misleading representations
by collectors, 182–184
Money center banks, 2–3
Motivating collectors,
253–256
phrases for, 89–91
Myths and games of
debtors, 143–153

N

Nailing down the promise
to pay, 98
National Association of
Credit Management,
50
Negative acknowledg-
ment, 130
Negotiation, collecting is,
12–13
Nierenberg, Gerald, 12
No collection policies,
7–8
No commitment answers,
147
Non-English speaking
debtor, 160
Notices in office, 88–89

O

Objections, bridging of,
133–135
Offensive tackle by
debtor, 145–146
Offer of payment,
56–57
Old accounts, 127–128
O'Neill, Tip, 258
Orthodontic bills,
224–225
Other companies, policies
of, 9–10
Outside collection services.
See Collection
agencies

Violations of agreement,
148–149
Visa payments, 55, 56

W

Wage earner's plans, 164
Wages. *See* Salaries
Weasel words, 37–38
Win-win negotiations,
12–13

Workers' compensation
claims, 173, 221–222
Writing off accounts, 116
Written communications,
83–92. *see also*
Statements
in hierarchy of commu-
nications, 133
motivating phrases for
collection, 89–91
samples of, 90–91